Accounting Euro Edition

Accounting
Euro Edition

Ursula Mooney

Gill & Macmillan

Gill & Macmillan
Hume Avenue
Park West
Dublin 12
with associated companies throughout the world
www.gillmacmillan.ie

© Ursula Mooney 2000

978 07171 3181 5

Print origination in Ireland by DTP Workshop

*The paper used in this book is made from the wood pulp of managed forests. For every
tree felled, at least one is planted, thereby renewing natural resources.*

CONTENTS

Introduction

This book is intended to cover the NCVA Level 2 course for Accounting and Accounts.

Section A

This section will provide students with the basic principles necessary to be able to prepare Final Accounts of small or medium types of organisations. It sets out the principles of double-entry Bookkeeping and explains the meaning and purpose of a Trial Balance.

Emphasis will be placed on items that appear as 'adjustments' to the Trial Balance, e.g. Depreciation, Accruals, Prepayments, Bad debts and Bad debts provisions. The double-entry system for these items is set out in separate chapters.

The section shows the layout of the Trading, Profit and Loss Account and the Balance Sheet, both of a sole trader and a limited company. It explains the meaning of accounting terms, such as Cost of sales, Gross profit, Net profit, Current assets, Current liabilities and Working capital. It also deals with such items as Intangible assets, Drawings, Long-term liabilities and Retained profits, etc.

There are practical exercises at the end of each chapter, bringing in the treatment of all the adjustments necessary to cover Section A of the NCVA examination paper.

Section B

This will introduce students to the interpretation of financial information and the calculation of accounting ratios. It explains each ratio and trains students to be able to make adequate comments on Financial Accounts.

The section compares actual and budgeted figures and enables students to project selling prices, etc.
It discusses Mark up and Gross profit percentage.

Cash budgets are explained and comments made on cash forecasts.

Projected Trading, Profit and Loss Accounts and Balance Sheets are shown and this will enable students to analyse figures and choose between alternative courses of action.

Practical exercises follow at the end of each chapter to prepare students for Section B of the NCVA examination paper.

Section C

This section will recap on questions of accounting terminology in order to fully prepare students for Section C of the NCVA examination paper.

The section concludes with three practice NCVA examination papers.

CHAPTER 1

Principles of the Double-entry System of Bookkeeping

Role of Accounting/Bookkeeping

Accounting is concerned with the preparation of financial information to help people make decisions. The people who use financial information include managers, employees, shareholders, potential purchasers, customers, banks, Government and suppliers. In order to be able to provide such information for these users, each business must keep an accurate record of its activities on a day-to-day basis.

Bookkeeping may be defined as the art of recording day-to-day transactions of a business in a monetary manner.

Accounting may be defined as the use of these day-to-day transactions and the preparation of Final Accounts in order to determine the profit or loss of a business over a period of time.

The Double-entry Principle

The name 'double-entry' suggests that every business transaction has a twofold aspect and that both sides must be recorded. This is best explained by an example: A, a retailer, sells a television to a customer for €200. This is one transaction but it has two distinct aspects. A has received €200 but has given the television to the customer. If we were preparing the accounts for A, we would have to record two transactions: (1) he has received €200, and (2) he has given away the television. It can be seen that double-entry is involved and this is fundamental to the whole theory of accounting.

A method of recording transactions such as the above is achieved through ledger accounts. Ledger accounts are commonly known as T-accounts because of the resemblance to the letter T when drawn up. Entries on the left-hand side are known as DEBIT entries (dr) and entries on the right-hand side are known as CREDIT entries (cr).

Before going on to consider examples of the double-entry system, some explanations are required.

Expense: an expense is any item of day-to-day expenditure that a business has to bear in order to function. Examples of such expenses are rent, rates, wages, insurance and light and heat.

Asset: an asset is something that a business owns or is owed. Examples are machinery, property, motor vehicles, stock, cash and debtors.

Liability: a liability is something that a business owes to others. Examples are creditors (money owed to suppliers where a business purchased goods on credit), bank overdraft and loans.

Income: income is money that a business receives during its trading activities. Examples are sales income as a result of selling goods to customers and rental income where a business has let out some of its property to tenants.

Gain: a gain is the excess of income over expenses such as the profit of a business for the period.

As mentioned earlier, each ledger account of a business has a Debit (left side) and a Credit (right side) thus:

LEDGER ACCOUNT

Debit			Credit		
Date	Details	Amount	Date	Details	Amount

One basic rule of bookkeeping when trying to understand the double-entry system is this:

All expenses and assets go on the DEBIT side of the ledger and all liabilities and income go on the CREDIT side of the ledger.

Debit Expenses and assets
Credit Liabilities and income/gains

Keeping this rule of double-entry in mind, you will not get too confused as to which side of the ledger a transaction goes.

We must introduce the concept of Capital here before we go on to give any examples of double-entry transactions.

Capital: it is the practice to think of the owner of the business as being separate from the business itself. When a person starts up a business and invests money in it i. e. Capital, the money belongs to the business and the business owes it to the owner. In accounting, it is the business's records that are presented. Capital is always treated as a liability as the business owes it to the owner. Therefore, the Capital account will always be credited.

For example, John Smith starts a business and invests €40,000. This goes into the Bank account of the business. The money is now the property of the business. The double-entry to record the transaction is:

Debit Bank account (asset)
Credit Capital account (liability)

BANK ACCOUNT

Debit					Credit
Jan. 1	Capital	40,000			

CAPITAL ACCOUNT

Debit						Credit
			Jan. 1	Bank		40,000

This means that the Capital account is a liability (the business owes John Smith €40,000) and the Bank account is an asset.

Let us now go through a few simple examples and open ledger accounts for each of them.

PRACTICE EXAMPLE 1

J. Norris is a retailer and has the following transactions:

Jan. 1: J. Norris introduces €30,000 cash as Capital into the business.

To record this, we need to open a Capital account and a Bank account. As already stated, Capital is a liability (the business owes J. Norris €30,000) so the double-entry is:
Debit Bank account (asset)
Credit Capital account (liability)

We assume in this case that the money is lodged to the bank account of the business. The entry is thus to debit the Bank account. However, if the money were kept as cash, the entry would be to debit the Cash account. Both bank and cash are assets of a business.

BANK ACCOUNT

Debit						Credit
Jan. 1	Capital	30,000				

CAPITAL ACCOUNT

Debit						Credit
			Jan. 1	Bank		30,000

J. Norris is now starting off his business with €30,000 lodged to the Bank account of his business.

Jan. 2: Purchased goods on credit from HX Supplies for €9,000.

To record this transaction in the ledger we must open an account for HX Supplies and a Purchases account. HX Supplies is a creditor and a liability as the business owes €9,000 for goods purchased but not yet paid for. The Purchases account is regarded as an expense account since effectively the business has incurred expenditure of €9,000 on goods that are for resale.

Keeping double-entry in mind we will:
Debit Purchases account (expense)
Credit HX Supplies (liability/creditor)

PURCHASES ACCOUNT

Debit						Credit
Jan. 2	HX Supplies	9,000				

HX SUPPLIES (CREDITOR)

Debit				Credit	
			Jan. 2	Purchases	9,000

From these ledger accounts we can see that J. Norris owes HX Supplies €9,000 and that there is an expense created in the form of Purchases of €9,000.

Jan. 4: Sold goods on credit to P. O'Mahony for €300.

To record this transaction in the ledger we must open an account for P. O'Mahony (customer) and a Sales account. Here P. O'Mahony owes the business €300 as he has not paid for the goods yet. P. O'Mahony is considered a debtor as he owes money to the business. As P. O'Mahony is a debtor to the business he can also be considered an asset. Remember, an asset is something that the business owns or is owed. The business has made a sale and this sale is treated as income. Keeping the rules of double-entry in mind we will:

Debit P. O'Mahony (asset/debtor)
Credit Sales account (income)

P. O'MAHONY (DEBTOR)

Debit				Credit	
Jan. 4	Sales	300			

SALES ACCOUNT

Debit				Credit	
			Jan. 4	P. O'Mahony	300

From these ledger accounts we can see that P. O'Mahony is a debtor to the business i. e. he owes the business €300. There is sales income to the value of €300 as the Sales account has a credit entry.

Jan. 10: Purchased a motor vehicle for use in the business for €3,000 and paid by cheque.

Here the business has acquired a motor vehicle which is an asset (remember, an asset is something that the business owns or is owed). The business paid for the vehicle on January 10 so it will have €3,000 less cash in its bank account. This means that the bank account will have to be reduced by €3,000. The money currently in the bank account is a debit entry (asset), so to reduce this amount the entry for the €3,000 will have to be a credit.

So the double-entry in the ledger will be:
Debit Motor vehicles account (asset)
Credit Bank account (reducing the amount of money in the bank account)

MOTOR VEHICLES ACCOUNT

Debit				Credit	
Jan. 10	Bank	3,000			

BANK ACCOUNT

Debit						Credit
Jan. 1	Capital	30,000	Jan. 10	Motor vehicles		3,000

Jan. 11: Purchased goods for €400, paid by cheque.

On this occasion the goods are paid for on January 11, the day of purchase. There is no need to create an account in the name of the supplier as the business does not owe any money to him.

The ledger accounts affected in this instance are the Purchases account and the Bank account. A purchase, as already stated, is an expense so there will be a debit entry in the Purchases account. The business will have €400 less money in its bank so the Bank account will have to be credited as the asset has been decreased.

It must be stressed that all assets and expenses go on the debit side of the ledger and all liabilities and income go on the credit side of the ledger. Decreases in assets or expenses go on the credit side of the ledger and decreases in liabilities or income go on the debit side of the ledger.

Debit Purchases account (expense)
Credit Bank account (reducing the money in the bank account)

PURCHASES ACCOUNT

Debit					Credit
Jan. 2	HX Supplies	9,000			
Jan. 11	Bank	400			

BANK ACCOUNT

Debit						Credit
Jan. 1	Capital	30,000	Jan. 10	Motor vehicles		3,000
			Jan. 11	Purchases		400

Jan. 15: Sold goods for €50 cash.

Here again, as the goods were paid for on the day of purchase by the customer, we do not need tocreate an account in the name of the customer as he does not owe the business any money. The ledger accounts required here are the Bank account and the Sales account. The sum of €50 is received into the bank account of the business so this suggests a debit entry in the Bank account. T hebusiness has created income in the form of sales so the entry in the Sales account is on the credit side.

Debit Bank account (asset - increasing the money in the bank)
Credit Sales account (income)

BANK ACCOUNT

Debit						Credit
Jan. 1	Capital	30,000	Jan. 10	Motor vehicles		3,000
Jan. 15	Sales	50	Jan. 11	Purchases		400

SALES ACCOUNT

Debit					Credit
			Jan. 4	P. O'Mahony	300
			Jan. 15	Bank	50

Jan. 18: Paid insurance €400 by cheque.

The ledger accounts needed here are an Insurance account and the Bank account. Insurance is an expense to the business so in the Insurance account the entry will be on the debit side. The credit entry will be in the Bank account.

Debit Insurance account (expense)
Credit Bank account (reducing the amount of money in the bank account)

INSURANCE ACCOUNT

Debit					Credit
Jan. 18	Bank	400			

BANK ACCOUNT

Debit					Credit
Jan. 1	Capital	30,000	Jan. 10	Motor vehicles	3,000
Jan. 15	Sales	50	Jan. 11	Purchases	400
			Jan. 18	Insurance	400

Jan. 20: Purchased machinery for use in the business on credit from KLM Ltd for €4,000.

The ledger accounts to be opened in this instance are a Machinery account and an account for KLM Ltd. Here the business has acquired an asset, machinery, so this account will be debited. The business owes KLM Ltd €4,000 so KLM Ltd is a creditor and this account will be credited.

Debit Machinery account (asset)
Credit KLM Ltd (creditor/liability)

MACHINERY ACCOUNT

Debit					Credit
Jan. 20	KLM Ltd	4,000			

KLM LTD (CREDITOR)

Debit					Credit
			Jan. 20	Machinery account	4,000

As these accounts show, the business now has an asset in the form of machinery worth €4,000 and owes KLM Ltd, a creditor, €4,000.

Balancing the Ledger Account

If we wish to know at any particular time what the net effects of the recorded transactions are, we must balance the ledger account. To do this we add up the amount on each side, subtract the lesser total from the greater and write in the difference or balance on the lesser side so that the two sides will now be equal. The balance will be 'carried down' (c/d) and dated the last day of the accounting period. It will also then be 'brought down' (b/d) usually dated the first day of the next accounting period, so that we can see at a glance the net effect of the transactions.

Let us now look at the Bank account to find out the balance as on February 1.

BANK ACCOUNT

Debit					Credit
Jan. 1	Capital	30,000	Jan. 10	Motor vehicles	3,000
Jan. 15	Sales	50	Jan. 11	Purchases	400
			Jan. 18	Insurance	400

As can be seen from the above Bank account, the business started off on January 1 with €30,000 Capital lodged by J. Norris, the owner. On January 10, €3,000 was withdrawn to pay for a motor vehicle. On January 11, €400 was withdrawn to pay for goods purchased. On January 15, €50 was received into the bank account as a result of a cash sale. On January 18, €400 was withdrawn to pay for insurance. If we balance this account we can see at a glance how much money the business has left at the start of the new accounting period on February 1.

BANK ACCOUNT

Debit					Credit
Jan. 1	Capital	30,000	Jan. 10	Motor vehicles	3,000
Jan. 15	Sales	50	Jan. 11	Purchases	400
			Jan. 18	Insurance	400
			Jan. 31	Balance c/d	26,250
		30,050			30,050
Feb. 1	Balance b/d	26,250			

In balancing the account you will notice that the entries on the debit side total €30,050. The entries on the credit side without the balancing figure come to €3,800. The difference is €26,250 and, as the debit side is the larger, it is a debit balance. The balance, i. e. the difference, of €26,250 has been entered on the credit side as at January 31. The letters 'c/d' have been placed after the word 'balance' meaning 'carried down'. The balance has been entered on the debit side as at February 1 below the total and the letters 'b/d' (brought down) written beside the word 'balance'. We can see that the business has €26,250 in its bank account as at February 1. It is, of course, b/d on the debit side. It is an asset to the business. If the balance were b/d on the credit side it would mean that the business was overdrawn in its bank account, i. e. it had a liability. This, of course, is not the case here.

Let us look at the other ledger accounts.

CAPITAL ACCOUNT

Debit					Credit
Jan. 31	Balance c/d	30,000	Jan. 1	Bank	30,000
			Feb. 1	Balance b/d	30,000

As at February 1, the business still has €30,000 capital. The owner of the business, J. Norris, has neither added to this capital nor withdrawn from it during the month of January. Later on when doing the final accounts of a business, we shall see that any profit earned by the business will increase the capital and any withdrawals by the owner will reduce the capital.

PURCHASES ACCOUNT

Debit					Credit
Jan. 2	HX Supplies	9,000			
Jan. 11	Bank	400			
		9,400			

The Purchases account is not balanced in the ordinary way. This total figure for purchases will be transferred into the Trading Account of the business. It will appear in the Trial Balance as a debit of €9,400. As we can see from this account, the total purchases for the month of January are €9,400.

HX SUPPLIES (CREDITOR)

Debit					Credit
Jan. 31	Balance c/d	9,000	Jan. 2	Purchases	9,000
			Feb. 1	Balance b/d	9,000

As at February 1, the business owes HX Supplies €9,000. There is a credit balance of €9,000 indicating a liability to the business.

P. O'MAHONY (DEBTOR)

Debit					Credit
Jan. 4	Sales	300	Jan. 31	Balance c/d	300
Feb. 1	Balance b/d	300			

As at February 1, there is a debit balance of €300. This means that P. O'Mahony owes the business €300 and so is an asset to the business.

SALES ACCOUNT

Debit					Credit
			Jan. 4	P. O'Mahony	300
			Jan. 15	Bank	50
					350

As with the Purchases account, the Sales account is not balanced in the ordinary way. The total sales figure of €350 will be transferred to the Trading Account. This figure will go into the Trial Balance as a credit entry. The Trading Account and the Trial Balance will be explained in later chapters.

MOTOR VEHICLES ACCOUNT

Debit						Credit
Jan. 10	Bank	3,000	Jan. 31	Balance c/d		3,000
Feb. 1	Balance b/d	3,000				

As at February 1, the business has an asset in the form of motor vehicles to the value of €3,000.

INSURANCE ACCOUNT

Debit						Credit
Jan. 18	Bank	400				

The Insurance account is not balanced in the ordinary way. This amount will eventually be transferred to the Profit and Loss Account of the business. It will appear in the Trial Balance on the debit side as an expense.

MACHINERY ACCOUNT

Debit						Credit
Jan. 20	KLM Ltd	4,000	Jan. 31	Balance c/d		4,000
Feb. 1	Balance b/d	4,000				

As at February 1, the business owns machinery to the value of €4,000, which is an asset.

KLM LTD (CREDITOR)

Debit						Credit
Jan. 31	Balance c/d	4,000	Jan. 20	Machinery		4,000
			Feb. 1	Balance b/d		4,000

As at February 1, there is a credit balance of €4,000 meaning that KLM Ltd is owed €4,000 by the business.

NOTE: You may wonder at this stage why some accounts are balanced in full and others are left without a balance being brought down. All the ledger accounts that will eventually go into the Balance Sheet are balanced in full, i. e. all the accounts that are classified as asset or liability accounts. These include such accounts as Debtors, Creditors, Machinery, Bank and Capital. All the ledger accounts that will eventually go into the Profit and Loss Account are not fully balanced, i. e. those accounts that are classified as expenses or income accounts. These include such accounts as Insurance, Purchases, Sales, Rent and Rates. This will become much clearer to you when you study the section on Final Accounts.

PRACTICE EXAMPLE 2

Draw up ledger accounts for the following transactions of P. Jacob, a retailer, for the month of January. Balance the ledger accounts bringing down the balances as at 1 February.

Jan. 1: P. Jacob introduced Capital of €50,000 into the business bank account.
Jan. 2: Purchased goods on credit from HM Ltd for €8,000.
Jan. 8: Sold goods for €900 cash.
Jan. 10: Sold goods on credit to P. Molloy for €860.
Jan. 13: Purchased machinery on credit from Dex Ltd for €4,000.
Jan. 15: Sold goods for €80 cash.
Jan. 20: Sold goods on credit to S. Smith for €930.
Jan. 21: Purchased goods on credit from Roche Ltd for €4,000.
Jan. 22: Paid rates €650 by cheque.
Jan. 23: Purchased typewriter for use in the business, paid €300 by cheque.
Jan. 26: Purchased goods for €400 cash.
NOTE: Assume all cash transactions are put through the Bank account.

PRACTICE EXAMPLE 2 SOLUTION

CAPITAL ACCOUNT (LIABILITY)

Debit					Credit
Jan. 31	Balance c/d	50,000	Jan. 1	Bank	50,000
			Feb. 1	Balance b/d	50,000

BANK ACCOUNT (ASSET)

Debit					Credit
Jan. 1	Capital	50,000	Jan. 22	Rates	650
Jan. 8	Sales	900	Jan. 23	Office equipment	300
Jan. 15	Sales	80	Jan. 26	Purchases	400
			Jan. 31	Balance b/d	49,630
		50,980			50,980
Feb. 1	Balance b/d	49,630			

PURCHASES ACCOUNT (EXPENSE)

Debit					Credit
Jan. 2	HM Ltd	8,000			
Jan. 21	Roche Ltd	4,000			
Jan. 26	Bank	400			
		12,400			

HM LTD (CREDITOR/LIABILITY)

Debit				Credit	
Jan. 31	Balance c/d	8,000	Jan. 2	Purchases	8,000
			Feb. 1	Balance b/d	8,000

SALES ACCOUNT (INCOME)

Debit				Credit	
			Jan. 8	Bank	900
			Jan. 10	P. Molloy	860
			Jan. 15	Bank	80
			Jan. 20	S. Smith	930
					2,770

P. MOLLOY (DEBTOR/ASSET)

Debit				Credit	
Jan. 10	Sales	860	Jan. 31	Balance c/d	860
Feb. 1	Balance b/d	860			

MACHINERY ACCOUNT (ASSET)

Debit				Credit	
Jan. 13	Dex Ltd	4,000	Jan. 31	Balance c/d	4,000
Feb. 1	Balance b/d	4,000			

DEX LTD (CREDITOR/LIABILITY)

Debit				Credit	
Jan. 31	Balance c/d	4,000	Jan. 13	Machinery	4,000
			Feb. 1	Balance b/d	4,000

S. SMITH (DEBTOR/ASSET)

Debit				Credit	
Jan. 20	Sales	930	Jan. 31	Balance c/d	930
Feb. 1	Balance b/d	930			

ROCHE LTD (CREDITOR/LIABILITY)

Debit				Credit	
Jan. 31	Balance c/d	4,000	Jan. 21	Purchases	4,000
			Feb. 1	Balance b/d	4,000

RATES ACCOUNT (EXPENSE)

Debit					Credit
Jan. 22	Bank	650			

OFFICE EQUIPMENT ACCOUNT (ASSET)

Debit					Credit
Jan. 23	Bank	300	Jan. 31	Balance c/d	300
Feb. 1	Balance b/d	300			

NOTES:

1. The Bank account is an asset account; all monies received go on the debit side and all monies withdrawn go on the credit side. The debit balance means that the business has €49,630 left in its bank account as on February 1st.

2. The Purchases account is an expense account so entries are always on the debit side. The account records both cash and credit purchases.

3. HM Ltd is a creditor i. e. a liability to the business. The balance of €8,000 means that the business owes HM Ltd €8,000.

4. The Sales account is an income account so entries are always on the credit side. This account records both cash and credit sales.

5. P. Molloy is a debtor i. e. an asset to the business and owes the business €860.

6. The Machinery account is an asset so the balance will always be on the debit side. The account shows that the business owns machinery to the value of €4,000.

7. Dex Ltd is a creditor since the business owes him €4,000.

8. S. Smith is a debtor and owes the business €930.

9. Roche Ltd is a creditor since the business owes him €4,000.

10. The Rates account is an expense account showing that the business had to pay €650 in rates.

11. The Office equipment account is an asset reflecting the purchase of a typewriter and the balance will always be on the debit side of this account.

Extension of the Double-entry System of Bookkeeping

We now know that each transaction has a twofold aspect, that is, there is always a debit entry and a credit entry in the ledger accounts. The advantage of this is that there is a complete record of each transaction. It is also possible to check the arithmetical accuracy of the work of the bookkeeper by extracting a Trial Balance which will be explained in Chapter 2. This will provide the information we need to prepare Final Accounts which will be discussed in Chapter 3.

There are many more transactions that occur in a typical business other than those explained earlier. For instance, customers return goods; the business returns goods to suppliers; customers pay for goods previously bought on credit; the business pays suppliers for goods; bad debts occur where a debtor fails to pay; discounts are given to customers and taken from suppliers and the owner of the business withdraws money for personal use. The examples which follow incorporate such transactions and will help you to fully grasp the double-entry system of bookkeeping.

Ledger accounts can be classified into different categories according to the nature of the transactions recorded in them.

Debtors ledger: this records the accounts of debtors or customers, i. e. people or firms who owe money to the business.

Creditors ledger: this records the accounts of creditors or suppliers, i. e. people or firms to whom the business owes money.

These two ledgers are also known as Personal Ledgers because they contain the accounts of persons or firms.

Nominal or General Ledger: this represents all the other ledger accounts of a business which are of a non-personal nature. Examples are Sales, Purchases, Machinery, Bank, Cash, Insurance, Rent, etc.

Let us work through a Practice Example bringing in as much of the double-entry system of bookkeeping as possible.

PRACTICE EXAMPLE 3

The following are the transactions of Mr Jones in January 1999.

Jan. 1: Introduced Capital into the bank account of the business, €50,000.
Debit Bank account, €50,000
Credit Capital account, €50,000

Jan. 4: Purchased equipment, paid by cheque €20,000.
Debit Equipment account, €20,000
Credit Bank account, €20,000

Jan. 8: Purchased goods on credit from Doyle Ltd, €8,000.
Debit Purchases account, €8,000
Credit Doyle Ltd, €8,000

Jan. 10: Sold goods on credit to R. Murphy, €440.
Debit R. Murphy, €440
Credit Sales account, €440

Jan. 12: Paid advertising by cheque, €200.
Debit Advertising account, €200
Credit Bank account, €200

Jan. 13 Cash sales, €480.
Debit Cash account, €480
Credit Sales account, €480

Jan. 14: R. Murphy paid the business €440 owed.
Debit Bank account, €440
Credit R. Murphy, €440

Jan. 16: Purchased goods on credit from Doyle Ltd €4,000.
Debit Purchases account, €4,000
Credit Doyle Ltd, €4,000

Jan. 20: Paid Doyle Ltd, €10,000.
Debit Doyle Ltd, €10,000
Credit Bank account, €10,000

Jan. 22: Purchased goods on credit from Hoskins & Co. for €1,500.
Debit Purchases account, €1,500
Credit Hoskins & Co. , €1,500

Jan. 23: Paid rent by cheque, €800.
Debit Rent account, €800
Credit Bank account, €800

Jan. 24: Returned goods to Hoskins & Co. to the value of €40.
Debit Hoskins & Co. , €40
Credit Purchases returns account, €40

NOTE: When a business returns goods previously purchased, the transaction is entered in a Purchases returns account on the credit side. The amount in this account will eventually reduce the figure for Purchases in the Final Accounts. It makes sense that if Purchases are always recorded on the debit side in the ledger, Purchases returns are always recorded on the credit side in order to reduce the Purchases figure. In the account of Hoskins & Co. , the credit will record the amount that is owed to Hoskins & Co. If the business returns goods to them, this will be recorded on the debit to reduce the amount owed.

Jan. 25: Sold goods on credit to K. Noble, €200.
Debit K. Noble, €200
Credit Sales account, €200

Jan. 26: The owner of the business, Mr Jones, withdrew €500 from the bank account of the business for his own personal use.
Debit Drawings account, €500
Credit Bank account, €500

NOTE: Withdrawals of money for private use are known as Drawings. The amount of Drawings at the end of the accounting period will reduce the capital of the business. At the moment the Capital is €50,000. If the owner takes out €500 for his own use this will bring down the capital to €49,500. The effect of this is shown in the Final Accounts. If Capital, being a liability, is on the credit side of the ledger, then Drawings are on the debit side in order to reduce the Capital.

Jan. 27: K. Noble returned goods to the value of €35.
Debit Sales returns account, €35.
Credit K. Noble, €35.

NOTE: When goods previously sold are returned by a customer, the entry appears in a Sales returns account as a debit. This amount will eventually reduce the Sales in the Final Accounts. As Sales are always on the credit side, any reduction in the form of returns will be on the debit side of the ledger. In K. Noble's account, the amount he owes the business is on the debit side since he is a debtor. If he returns goods to the value of €35, this amount will be credited to his account, thus reducing what he owes.

Jan. 28: Purchased goods on credit from Dalton Ltd, €1,000.
Debit Purchases account, €1,000
Credit Dalton Ltd, €1,000

Jan. 29: Paid Dalton Ltd €950 and received €50 discount, thus clearing the account.
Debit Dalton Ltd, €950 + €50 = €1,000
Credit Bank account, €950
Credit Discount received account, €50

NOTE: Dalton Ltd was a creditor to the business to the value of €1,000. The business paid €950 to Dalton so the entry for this is to debit Dalton Ltd and to credit the Bank account. The €50 still outstanding to Dalton Ltd is given in the form of discount to the business. This is classified as income for the business. A Discount received account is opened and the €50 is credited to this account. The debit entry for this €50 is in Dalton Ltd account, thus reducing the balance on this account to zero.

Jan. 30: Sold goods on credit to K. Noble for €80.
Debit K. Noble, €80
Credit Sales account, €80

Jan. 31: K. Noble cleared his account and was allowed 5% discount.
Debit Bank account, €233
Debit Discount allowed account, €12
Credit K. Noble, €233 + €12 = €245

NOTE: K. Noble's account as at January 30 shows that he owes the business €280 - €35 = €245. The business is allowing him 5% discount which is €245 @ 5% = €12 approx. As a result K. Noble will pay the business €245 - €12 = €233. The double-entry to record the payment by K. Noble of €233 is to debit the Bank account and credit K. Noble. The discount allowed of €12 is classified as an expense to the business. A Discount allowed account is opened and the €12 is debited to this account. The credit entry for this €12 is in K. Noble's account thus reducing his balance to zero.

We will now present the ledger accounts of the above transactions. Study each entry carefully so that you understand the double-entry system.

LEDGER ACCOUNTS OF MR JONES' BUSINESS

BANK ACCOUNT

Debit						Credit
Jan. 1	Capital	50,000	Jan. 4	Equipment		20,000
Jan. 14	R. Murphy	440	Jan. 12	Advertising		200
Jan. 31	K. Noble	233	Jan. 20	Doyle Ltd		10,000
			Jan. 23	Rent		800
			Jan. 26	Drawings		500
			Jan. 29	Dalton Ltd		950
			Jan. 31	Balance c/d		18,223
		50,673				50,673
Feb. 1	Balance b/d	18,223				

CAPITAL ACCOUNT

Debit					Credit
Jan. 31	Balance c/d	50,000	Jan. 1	Bank	50,000
			Feb. 1	Balance b/d	50,000

EQUIPMENT ACCOUNT

Debit					Credit
Jan. 4	Bank	20,000	Jan. 31	Balance c/d	20,000
Feb. 1	Balance b/d	20,000			

PURCHASES ACCOUNT

Debit					Credit
Jan. 8	Doyle Ltd	8,000			
Jan. 16	Doyle Ltd	4,000			
Jan. 22	Hoskins & Co.	1,500			
Jan. 28	Dalton Ltd	1,000			
		14,500			

CREDITORS LEDGER
DOYLE LTD

Debit			Credit		
Jan. 20	Bank	10,000	Jan. 8	Purchases	8,000
			Jan. 16	Purchases	4,000
Jan. 31	Balance c/d	2,000			
		12,000			12,000
			Feb. 1	Balance b/d	2,000

DEBTORS LEDGER
R. MURPHY

Debit			Credit		
Jan. 10	Sales	440	Jan. 14	Bank	440

SALES ACCOUNT

Debit			Credit		
			Jan. 10	R. Murphy	440
			Jan. 13	Cash	480
			Jan. 25	K. Noble	200
			Jan. 30	K. Noble	80
					1,200

ADVERTISING ACCOUNT

Debit			Credit		
Jan. 12	Bank	200			

CASH ACCOUNT

Debit			Credit		
Jan. 13	Sales	480	Jan. 31	Balance c/d	480
Feb. 1	Balance b/d	480			

CREDITORS LEDGER
HOSKINS & CO.

Debit			Credit		
Jan. 24	Purchases returns	40	Jan. 22	Purchases	1,500
Jan. 31	Balance c/d	1,460			
		1,500			1,500
			Feb. 1	Balance b/d	1,460

RENT ACCOUNT

Debit						Credit
Jan. 23	Bank	800				

PURCHASES RETURNS ACCOUNT

Debit						Credit
			Jan. 24	Hoskins & Co.		40

DEBTORS LEDGER
K. NOBLE

Debit						Credit
Jan. 25	Sales	200	Jan. 27	Sales returns		35
Jan. 30	Sales	80	Jan. 31	Bank		233
			Jan. 31	Discount allowed		12
		280				280

DRAWINGS ACCOUNT

Debit						Credit
Jan. 26	Bank	500				

SALES RETURNS ACCOUNT

Debit						Credit
Jan. 27	K. Noble	35				

CREDITORS LEDGER
DALTON LTD

Debit						Credit
Jan. 29	Bank	950	Jan. 28	Purchases		1,000
Jan. 29	Discount received	50				
		1,000				1,000

DISCOUNT RECEIVED ACCOUNT

Debit						Credit
			Jan. 29	Dalton Ltd		50

DISCOUNT ALLOWED ACCOUNT

Debit						Credit
Jan. 31	K. Noble	12				

NOTES ON BALANCES:

1. Bank account: debit balance of €18,223 denotes that the business has this money in the bank as at February 1st. This is an asset to the business and will appear in the debit column of the Trial Balance which will be discussed in Chapter 2.

2. Capital account: this is a liability to the business of €50,000. The drawings by the owner, Mr Jones, will be deducted from this figure in the Final Accounts. This Capital will appear in the credit column of the Trial Balance.

3. Equipment account: there is a debit balance of €20,000 denoting an asset to the business. This will appear in the debit column of the Trial Balance.

4. Purchases account: the total purchases of €14,500 are an expense to the business and will appear in the debit column of the Trial Balance. There is no need to balance this account.

5. Doyle Ltd: the business owes Doyle Ltd €2,000 as at February 1st. This is a creditor/ liability to the business and will appear in the credit column of the Trial Balance.

6. R. Murphy: this debtor has paid his account in full. There is no closing balance so it will not appear in the Trial Balance.

7. Sales account: the total sales/income of the business is €1,200 and will appear in the credit column of the Trial Balance. There is no need to balance this account.

8. Advertising: the expense of advertising is €200 and will appear in the debit column of the Trial Balance. There is no need to balance this account.

9. Cash account: the business has €480 cash in hand which is an asset and will appear in the debit column of the Trial Balance.

10. Hoskins & Co. : this is a creditor/liability to the business of €1,460. This will appear in the credit column of the Trial Balance.

11. Rent account: the business has incurred an expense of €800 which will appear in the debit column of the Trial Balance. There is no need to balance this account.

12. Purchases returns account: this shows a credit of €40 which will be subtracted from Purchases in the Final Accounts. It will appear in the credit column of the Trial Balance. There is no need to balance this account.

13. K. Noble: This debtor/asset has paid his account in full. The account will not appear in the Trial Balance as it shows no balance.

14. Drawings account: this amount will be subtracted from Capital in the Final Accounts. It will appear in the debit column of the Trial Balance. There is no need to balance this account.

15. Sales returns account: this figure will be subtracted from Sales in the Final Accounts and will appear in the debit column in the Trial Balance. There is no need to balance this account.

16. Dalton Ltd: this creditor/liability has no balance in its account as the business has paid it in full. The account will not appear in the Trial Balance.

17. Discount received account: this is income for the business and will appear in the credit column of the Trial Balance. There is no need to balance this account.

18. Discount allowed: this is an expense to the business and will appear in the debit column of the Trial Balance. There is no need to balance this account.

All ledger accounts that are classified as assets and liabilities are balanced in full and will appear in the Balance Sheet of the business at the end of the accounting period. All ledger accounts that are classified as expenses and income need not be balanced as they are transferred to the Profit and Loss Account of the business at the end of the accounting period. You need not worry about the Profit and Loss Account or Balance Sheet at this stage as these will be discussed in later chapters. But all ledger accounts that have a closing balance will appear in the Trial Balance which is the subject of Chapter 2.

Summary

In your study of double-entry so far, you must always remember that every accounting entry is based on the double-entry principle. If you realise that there are two aspects to every transaction will find accounting easier to understand. The basic rule is:

DEBIT Assets and expenses

CREDIT Liabilities and income

The converse of this is also true. If a business wanted to reduce an asset or an expense, the entry would be on the credit side of the asset or expense account. If it wanted to reduce a liability or income, the entry would be on the debit side of the liability or income account.

It follows that if all the debits and credits are entered correctly in the ledger, at the end of the accounting period the total of the debits will equal the total of the credits. The extraction and listing of balances in this way is called a Trial Balance. It is from this Trial Balance that Final Accounts are prepared, i. e. a Trading Account, Profit and Loss Account and Balance Sheet. These Final Accounts will be discussed in Chapter 3.

EXERCISE 1

Draw up and balance the ledger accounts of Robert Brown for the month of May 2000.
May 1: Introduced Capital, €80,000.
May 2: Purchased goods on credit from John Rea for €2,500.
May 3: Sold goods for €410 cash which was lodged to the bank.
May 4: Paid wages by cheque, €800.
May 5: Paid rent by cheque, €400.
May 8: Cash sales, €860.
May 9: Purchased goods, paid by cheque, €930.
May 10: Paid John Rea €2,000 by cheque.
May 12: Purchased goods, paid by cheque, €860.
May 13: Cash sales, €100.
May 15: Paid wages by cheque, €400.
May 17: Sold goods on credit to K. Doyle for €180.
May 19: K. Doyle returned goods to the value of €25.
May 27: Paid insurance by cheque, €390.

EXERCISE 2

Draw up and balance the ledger accounts of P. Hunter for the month of June 2000.

June 1: Introduced Capital, €95,000.
June 2: Purchased goods on credit from Robert & Co. for €8,000.
June 3: Cash Sales, €150, keeping money as cash in a cash account.
June 5: Sold goods on credit to P. Fox for €96.
June 6: Cash Purchases, €20.
June 8: Purchased goods on credit from Robert & Co. for €1,600.
June 9: Paid Robert & Co. €7,000 by cheque.
June 11: Paid wages, €960, by cheque.
June 12: Paid wages out of cash, €80.
June 15: Sold goods on credit to S. Roche for €1,600.
June 17: S. Roche returned goods, €700.
June 19: P. Fox paid €90 and was allowed €6 discount to clear his account.
June 22: Paid light and heat by cheque, €400.
June 23: Purchased delivery van by cheque, €8,000.
June 25: S. Roche cleared his account and was allowed 5% discount.
June 27: Paid wages by cheque, €820.
June 28: Cash Sales, €1,000, kept as cash.
June 29: Drawings by cheque, €450.
June 30: Paid wages by cheque, €820.

CHAPTER 2

Preparation of a Trial Balance from Ledger Accounts

We have seen how ledger accounts are written up and balanced in Chapter 1. You will recall how the total of all the debit balances equals the total of all the credit balances. The Trial Balance tests this. It is not an account, merely a checking device for the arithmetical accuracy of the transfer of transactions to the ledger accounts. It is not an integral part of the double-entry system. In a Trial Balance the debit balances from the ledger are listed in one column and the credit balances in another column. When all the entries have been made the total of the debit column should equal the total of the credit.

The attainment of a balanced Trial Balance only ensures that for every debit there is a corresponding credit, and vice versa. It does not ensure that transactions are posted to the correct accounts. For example, if a transaction were debited to the wrong account, this would not show up in the Trial Balance. If a transaction were omitted entirely from the accounts, leaving out both debit and credit entries, the Trial Balance would still balance although it would clearly be incorrect.

The Trial Balance is prepared with two columns, debit and credit, as shown below.)

TRIAL BALANCE OF.......................AS AT...................

Name of Account	Debit €	Credit €

Let us prepare a Trial Balance from the ledger accounts of P. Jacob (Practice Example 2 of Chapter 1):

CAPITAL ACCOUNT (LIABILITY)

Debit						Credit
Jan. 31	Balance c/d	50,000	Jan. 1	Bank	50,000
			Feb. 1	Balance b/d	50,000

BANK ACCOUNT (ASSET)

Debit				Credit
Jan. 1	Capital	50,000	Jan. 22	Rates	650
Jan. 8	Sales	900	Jan. 23	Office equip.	300
Jan. 15	Sales	80	Jan. 26	Purchases	400
			Jan. 31	Balance c/d	49,630
		50,980			50,980
Feb. 1	Balance b/d	49,630			

PURCHASES ACCOUNT (EXPENSE)

Debit				Credit
Jan. 2	HM Ltd	8,000		
Jan. 21	Roche Ltd	4,000		
Jan. 26	Bank	400		
		12,400		

HM LTD (CREDITOR/LIABILITY)

Debit				Credit
Jan. 31	Balance c/d	8,000	Jan. 2	Purchases	8,000
			Feb. 1	Balance b/d	8,000

SALES ACCOUNT (INCOME)

Debit				Credit
			Jan. 8	Bank	900
			Jan. 10	P. Molloy	860
			Jan. 15	Bank	80
			Jan. 20	S.Smith	930
					2,770

P. MOLLOY (DEBTOR)

Debit				Credit
Jan. 10	Sales	860	Jan. 31	Balance c/d	860
Feb. 1	Balance b/d	860			

MACHINERY ACCOUNT (ASSET)

Debit				Credit
Jan. 13	Dex Ltd	4,000	Jan. 31	Balance c/d	4,000
Feb. 1	Balance b/d	4,000			

DEX LTD (CREDITOR/LIABILITY)

Debit						Credit
Jan. 31	Balance c/d	4,000	Jan. 13	Machinery		4,000
			Feb. 1	Balance b/d		4,000

S. SMITH (DEBTOR/ASSET)

Debit						Credit
Jan. 20	Sales	930	Jan. 31	Balance c/d		930
Feb. 1	Balance b/d	930				

ROCHE LTD (CREDITOR/LIABILITY)

Debit						Credit
Jan. 31	Balance c/d	4,000	Jan. 21	Purchases		4,000
			Feb. 1	Balance b/d		4,000

RATES ACCOUNT (EXPENSE)

Debit						Credit
Jan. 22	Bank	650				

OFFICE EQUIPMENT ACCOUNT (ASSET)

Debit						Credit
Jan. 23	Bank	300	Jan. 31	Balance c/d		300
Feb. 1	Balance b/d	300				

TRIAL BALANCE OF P. JACOB AS AT 31 JANUARY

		Debit €	Credit €
Capital			50,000
Bank		49,630	
Purchases		12,400	
Sales			2,770
Creditors:	HM Ltd		8,000
	Dex Ltd		4,000
	Roche Ltd		4,000
Debtors:	P. Molloy	860	
	S. Smith	930	
Machinery		4,000	
Rates		650	
Office equipment		300	
		€68,770	€68,770

As in this example, the debit and credit columns of the Trial Balance are added up and the totals should agree.

The preparation of a complete set of accounts can be quite time-consuming. In examinations, questions on ledger accounts generally deal with only a relatively small part of the overall process. Examiners tend to give a Trial Balance for a business, taken out on the last day of the year, together with a list of adjustments and ask the student to prepare a set of Final Accounts from this information. The Trial Balance is a summary of the ledger accounts at the end of an accounting period before any adjustments have been made. It is from this Trial Balance that the Final Accounts are prepared, that is the Trading, Profit and Loss Account and Balance Sheet. It is on this format that Question 1 of the NCVA Accounting paper is based. This does not mean that you do need not to understand ledger accounts. You will need an understanding of double-entry in order to deal with adjustments to a Trial Balance given in an examination paper and to fully understand Final Accounts.

When preparing Final Accounts from a Trial Balance, all the income and expenses of the period must be transferred to the Trading, Profit and Loss Account, subject to any adjustments. Net profit and drawings must be transferred to the Capital Account. This enables you to compile the Balance Sheet. The preparation of these Final Accounts from the Trial Balance will be fully discussed in Chapter 3.

Let us now prepare a Trial Balance from the ledger accounts of Mr Jones (Practice Example 3, Chapter 1).

BANK ACCOUNT

Debit					Credit
Jan. 1	Capital	50,000	Jan. 4	Equipment	20,000
Jan. 14	R. Murphy	440	Jan. 12	Advertising	200
Jan. 31	K. Noble	233	Jan. 20	Doyle Ltd	10,000
			Jan. 23	Rent	800
			Jan. 26	Drawings	500
			Jan. 29	Dalton Ltd	950
			Jan. 31	Balance c/d	18,223
		50,673			50,673
Feb. 1	Balance b/d	18,223			

CAPITAL ACCOUNT

Debit					Credit
Jan. 31	Balance c/d	50,000	Jan. 1	Bank	50,000
			Feb. 1	Balance b/d	50,000

EQUIPMENT ACCOUNT

Debit					Credit
Jan. 4	Bank	20,000	Jan. 31	Balance c/d	20,000
Feb. 1	Balance b/d	20,000			

PURCHASES ACCOUNT

Debit					Credit
Jan. 8	Doyle Ltd	8,000			
Jan. 16	Doyle Ltd	4,000			
Jan. 22	Hoskins & Co.	1,500			
Jan. 28	Dalton Ltd	1,000			
		14,500			

CREDITORS LEDGER
DOYLE LTD

Debit					Credit
Jan. 20	Bank	10,000	Jan. 8	Purchases	8,000
			Jan. 16	Purchases	4,000
Jan. 31	Balance c/d	2,000			
		12,000			12,000
			Feb. 1	Balance b/d	2,000

DEBTORS LEDGER
R. MURPHY

Debit			Credit
Jan. 10	Sales	440	Jan. 14	Bank	440

SALES ACCOUNT

Debit			Credit
			Jan. 10	R. Murphy	440
			Jan. 13	Cash	480
			Jan. 25	K. Noble	200
			Jan. 30	K. Noble	80
					1,200

ADVERTISING ACCOUNT

Debit			Credit
Jan. 12	Bank	200			

CASH ACCOUNT

Debit			Credit
Jan. 13	Sales	480	Jan. 31	Balance c/d	480
Feb. 1	Balance b/d	480			

CREDITORS LEDGER
HOSKINS & CO.

Debit			Credit
Jan. 24	Purchases returns	40	Jan. 22	Purchases	1,500
Jan. 31	Balance c/d	1,460			
		1,500			1,500
			Feb. 1	Balance b/d	1,460

RENT ACCOUNT

Debit			Credit
Jan. 23	Bank	800			

PURCHASES RETURNS ACCOUNT

Debit			Credit
			Jan. 24	Hoskins & Co.	40

DEBTORS LEDGER
K. NOBLE

Debit					Credit
Jan. 25	Sales	200	Jan. 27	Sales returns	35
Jan. 30	Sales	80	Jan. 31	Bank	233
			Jan. 31	Discount allowed	12
		280			280

DRAWINGS ACCOUNT

Debit					Credit
Jan. 26	Bank	500			

SALES RETURNS ACCOUNT

Debit					Credit
Jan. 27	K. Noble	35			

CREDITORS LEDGER
DALTON LTD

Debit					Credit
Jan. 29	Bank	950	Jan. 28	Purchases	1,000
Jan. 29	Discount received	50			
		1,000			1,000

DISCOUNT RECEIVED ACCOUNT

Debit					Credit
			Jan. 29	Dalton Ltd	50

DISCOUNT ALLOWED ACCOUNT

Debit					Credit
Jan. 31	K. Noble	12			

TRIAL BALANCE OF MR JONES AS AT 31 JANUARY

	Debit €	Credit €
Capital		50,000
Bank	18,223	
Equipment	20,000	
Purchases	14,500	
Sales		1,200
Creditors: Doyle Ltd		2,000
Hoskins & Co.		1,460
Advertising	200	
Cash	480	
Rent	800	
Purchases returns		40
Sales returns	35	
Drawings	500	
Discount received		50
Discount allowed	12	
	€54,750	€54,750

In a Trial Balance, all assets and expenses are in the debit column and all liabilities and income are in the credit column. Items that reduce a debit will go into the credit column, and items that reduce a credit will go into the debit column.

Here is a _pro forma_ Trial Balance and you should study it carefully:

TRIAL BALANCE OF .... AS AT ....

	Debit €	Credit €
Purchases	x	
Purchases returns		x
Sales		x
Sales returns	x	
Stock	x	
Machinery	x	
Premises	x	
Bank (bank overdraft)	x	(x)
Cash	x	
Light and heat	x	
Salaries and wages	x	
Advertising	x	
Bank interest and charges	x	
Discount allowed	x	
Discount received		x
Carriage in	x	
Carriage out	x	
Debtors	x	
Creditors		x
Drawings	x	
Capital		x
	€ xxxx	€ xxxx

NOTE: All assets and expenses are in the debit column and all liabilities and income are in the credit column. Usually when preparing a Trial Balance for the purpose of Final Accounts, all debtors are grouped by means of an account called a Debtors Control Account. Simlarly, all creditors are grouped together in a Creditors Control Account. This is for practical purposes as a business may have hundreds of debtors and creditors and it would not be possible to list each one of them in a Trial Balance.

The Bank figure in a Trial Balance may be on either the debit or credit side. If the business has money in its bank account (an asset), this will be stated on the debit column. If it is overdrawn (a liability), the figure will appear on the credit column.

Carriage in represents an expense to the business, being the cost of delivering goods from suppliers. *Carriage out* is also an expense, being the cost of delivering goods to its customers.

The stock figure represents the stock of goods for sale the business has as an asset at the beginning of its accounting year. The figure is for opening stock i.e. stock remaining unsold from last year. The closing stock figure i.e. stock left unsold at the end of accounting year, will appear as one of the adjustments to the Trial Balance. This will be explained further in Chapter 3.

EXERCISE 1

Draw up the Trial Balance for Robert Brown for the month of May 2000. You will find these ledger accounts in Chapter 1, Exercise 1.

EXERCISE 2

Draw up the Trial Balance for P. Hunter for the month of June 2000. You will find these ledger accounts in Chapter 1, Exercise 2.

CHAPTER 3

Trading, Profit and Loss Account and Balance Sheet

Trading, Profit and Loss Account

The main reason for having a bookkeeping system is to build up accounting information to ascertain whether a business is making a profit or loss. The ultimate objective of accounting is to prepare a set of Final Accounts which consists of a Trading, Profit and Loss Account and a Balance Sheet.

A **Trading Account** is prepared in order to show the difference between Sales and the Cost of sales. Cost of sales is the purchase price of goods plus other direct expenses involved in the purchase of goods, such as Carriage in, customs duty, excise duty, etc.

The difference between Sales and the Cost of sales is known as Gross profit.

A **Profit and Loss Account** is prepared to show the difference between Gross profit and Expenses. These expenses include all expenses of a revenue nature that a business necessarily incurs (other than Cost of sales) in the running of its business. Examples are rent, rates, insurance, wages, etc.

The difference between Gross profit and Expenses is known as Net profit or Net loss.

PRACTICE EXAMPLE 1

The following is a Trial Balance extracted from the books of Martin Walsh as at 31 December 2000:

TRIAL BALANCE AS AT 31 DECEMBER 2000

	Debit €	Credit €
Opening stock	3,500	
Purchases	18,000	
Purchases returns		1,500
Carriage in	3,000	
Sales		27,500
Sales returns	1,000	
Light and heat	500	
Rent	750	
Insurance	250	
Wages	2,000	
	€29,000	€29,000

Closing stock as at 31 December 2000 is valued at €2,700.

Let us now first prepare a Trading Account for Martin Walsh.

TRADING ACCOUNT OF MARTIN WALSH FOR Y/E 31 DECEMBER 2000

	Debit €	Credit €
Sales	27,500	
less Sales returns	(1,000)	26,500
less Cost of Sales:		
Opening stock (1 Jan. 96)		3,500
Purchases	18,000	
less Purchases returns	(1,500)	16,500
Carriage in		3,000
Cost of goods available for sale		23,000
less Closing stock		(2,700)
= Cost of Sales		(20,300)
Gross profit		€6,200

GUIDANCE NOTES

1. The Trading Account comprises Sales less Cost of Sales to arrive at a figure for Gross profit of €6,200. In our double-entry examples in previous chapters, we assumed that all stock purchased for resale had been sold within the accounting period. In practice, this would not be the case. Most businesses do not sell all their stock within the accounting period, i.e. there is stock remaining unsold at the end of the year which will be carried forward and sold the following year. The closing stock figure of €2,700 represents stock that is not sold in 2000, but will be carried forward and sold in 2001. The opening stock of €3,500 represents stock unsold at the end of 1999 which is now carried forward and sold in this, the next accounting year, 2000. In other words, the opening stock of 2000 will have been the closing stock at the end of the last accounting period, 1999.

2. Carriage in is the cost of delivering the goods from the supplier to the business. This increases the cost of the goods purchased and so is added to the Purchases figure in the Trading Account.

3. Purchase returns and Sales returns are deducted from the totals for Purchases and Sales respectively in order to obtain the net amounts.

4. When calculating the Cost of Sales, the opening stock is added to net purchases (plus Carriage in). This figure represents the value of the goods the business *could* sell, i.e. €23,000.
   The closing stock figure of €2,700 represents the value of goods that remain unsold at the end of the year. Therefore, the value of goods the business *actually* sold is €23,000 - €2,700 = €20,300. This is the Cost of Sales. The Cost of Sales figure is then deducted from the net Sales figure to arrive at Gross profit.

Let us now prepare a Profit and Loss Account for Martin Walsh for y/e 31 December 2000:

PROFIT AND LOSS ACCOUNT OF MARTIN WALSH FOR Y/E 31 DECEMBER 2000

	Debit	Credit
	€	€
Gross profit		6,200
less Expenses:		
Light and heat	500	
Rent	750	
Insurance	250	
Wages	2,000	
		(3,500)
Net profit		€2,700

GUIDANCE NOTES

1. The Gross profit of €6,200 is transferred from the Trading Account to the credit side of the Profit and Loss Account. In order to arrive at Net profit, all expenses of the business are deducted from the Gross profit figure. If there were any gains such as discount received or rental income received for example, these would be credited to the Profit and Loss Account, that is, added to the Gross profit. The resulting Net profit of €2,700 is transferred to the credit side of the Capital account, thus increasing the owner's capital in the business. We will see this done later in the Balance Sheet.

2. Both the Trading Account and Profit and Loss Accounts are generally prepared with debit and credit columns. The double-entry principle applies here: all expenses/losses go in the debit column and all items of income/profit go in the credit column.

The Balance Sheet

A Balance Sheet is a statement of the assets and liabilities of a business at a particular date, usually at the end of the accounting year. In contrast, the Trading, Profit and Loss Account records expenses and income to arrive at Net profit.

The Balance Sheet contains a list of all the asset accounts from the ledger, such as machinery, premises, cash, bank, debtors. It also contains all the liabilities from the ledger, such as creditors, bank overdraft, capital, etc. The Balance Sheet acts as a check on the arithmetical accuracy of the accounts - assets should equal liabilities.

The Trading, Profit and Loss Account and Balance Sheet are prepared from the Trial Balance. All the expenses and income from the Trial Balance are transferred to the Trading, Profit and Loss Account and all assets and liabilities are transferred to the Balance Sheet. The balance of the Trading Account, i.e. Gross profit, is carried to the Profit and Loss Account. The balance of the Profit and Loss Account, i.e. Net profit, is carried to the Capital account in the Balance Sheet.

You must be sure to note that only expenditure of a revenue nature is charged to the Trading, Profit and Loss Account i.e. rent, wages, rates, etc. Expenditure of a capital nature is capitalised as an asset and is shown in the Balance Sheet. Examples of expenditure of a capital nature include purchase of machinery, vehicles, premises, etc. The difference between capital and revenue expenditure is discussed in more detail in Chapter 4.

PRACTICE EXAMPLE 2

Let us prepare a Trading, Profit and Loss Account and Balance Sheet for Mr Moore for year ending 31 December 2000 from the following Trial Balance:

TRIAL BALANCE OF MR MOORE FOR Y/E 31 DECEMBER 2000

	Debit €	Credit €
Opening stock	9,500	
Purchases	27,000	
Purchases returns		800
Sales		69,000
Sales returns	250	
Rent and rates	800	
Light and heat	1,600	
Wages and salaries	9,000	
Discount allowed	400	
Discount received		560
Carriage in	200	
Carriage out	350	
Plant and equipment	7,000	
Motor vehicles	16,000	
Debtors	28,000	
Creditors		8,000
Bank	11,000	
Cash	500	
Drawings	2,200	
Capital		35,440
	€113,800	€113,800

Closing stock is valued at €8,000.

PRACTICE EXAMPLE 2 SOLUTION

TRADING, PROFIT AND LOSS ACCOUNT OF MR MOORE FOR Y/E 31 DECEMBER 2000

	Debit €	Debit €	Credit €
Sales	69,000		
less Sales returns	(250)		68,750
less Cost of sales:			
Opening stock (1 Jan. 1996)		9,500	
Purchases	27,000		
less Purchases returns	(800)	26,200	
Carriage in		200	
Cost of goods available for sale:		35,900	
less Closing stock		(8,000)	
= Cost of sales:			(27,900)
Gross profit			40,850
Discount received			560
less Expenses:			41,410
Rent and rates		800	
Light and heat		1,600	
Wages and salaries		9,000	
Discount allowed		400	
Carriage out		350	
			(12,150)
Net profit			€29,260

BALANCE SHEET OF MR MOORE Y/E 31 DECEMBER 2000

	Debit €	Credit €
FIXED ASSETS		
Plant and equipment		7,000
Motor vehicles		16,000
		23,000
CURRENT ASSETS		
Closing stock	8,000	
Debtors	28,000	
Bank	11,000	
Cash	500	
	47,500	
less CURRENT LIABILITIES		
Creditors	(8,000)	
Working capital		39,500
		€62,500
Financed by:		
Capital	35,440	
Add Net profit	29,260	
	64,700	
less Drawings	(2,200)	
		€62,500

GUIDANCE NOTES

1. Assets are split in the Balance Sheet between Fixed and Current assets.

    Fixed assets: these are assets acquired for use within a business which are not for resale.

    Current assets: these are assets acquired for conversion into cash in the ordinary course of business.

    Current liabilities: these are amounts owed by a business which are expected to become payable within a year from the date of the Balance Sheet.

    Working capital: this is sometimes referred to as Net current assets, being the difference between Current assets and Current liabilities. When Current assets are greater than Current liabilities, the business is said to be in a liquid position, i.e. it is able to pay its Current liabilities in the short-term out of the funds in its Current assets. If Current liabilities are greater than the Current assets, the business has a Working capital deficit, i.e. it does not have enough funds in its Current assets to pay for its Current liabilities.

    The fixed assets figure in the Balance Sheet is added to the Working capital figure to give the total assets of the business, in this case €62,500.

2. **Financed by:** this section is sometimes called the proprietor's interest. It comprises the owner's interest in the business, i.e. the capital increased by Net profit earned and reduced by the drawings of the owner. Capital is a liability to the business. It represents what a business owes to its owner, that is the original investment, plus profit ploughed back, less drawings.

3. Note that every item in the Trial Balance goes once into the Trading Account or Profit and Loss Account or Balance Sheet. If an item is a debit in the Trial Balance, it is also a debit in the Trading Account or Profit and Loss account. Asset items in the Trial Balance appear as either Fixed assets or Current assets in the Balance Sheet. Liability items in the Trial Balance are shown under liabilities in the Balance Sheet. The closing stock figure which appears as an adjustment to the Trial Balance is entered twice - once in the Trading Account and once in the Balance Sheet as a Current asset. The closing stock figure is arrived at by a physical count of the goods unsold at the end of the year.

There are many more adjustments to the Trial Balance such as accruals and prepayments, depreciation of fixed assets etc., which will be discussed in later chapters.

EXERCISE 1

From the following Trial Balance of A. Cross, prepare a Trading, Profit and Loss Account and Balance Sheet as at 31 December 2000:

TRIAL BALANCE OF A. CROSS Y/E 31 DECEMBER 2000

	Debit €	Credit €
Purchases	22,000	
Sales		49,000
Purchases returns		400
Sales returns	590	
Office expenses	410	
Rates	860	
Salaries	1,900	
Commission	500	
Repairs	900	
Machinery	8,000	
Vehicles	4,900	
Debtors	16,000	
Creditors		8,200
Carriage in	400	
Carriage out	900	
Discount allowed	560	
Discount received		20
Bank overdraft		4,000
Cash in hand	860	
Opening stock	5,000	
Advertising	810	
Buildings	14,900	
Drawings	800	
Capital		18,670
	€80,290	€80,290

Closing stock at 31 2000 is €4,800.

EXERCISE 2

From the following Trial Balance of R. Ryan, prepare a Trading, Profit and Loss Account and Balance Sheet as at 30 June 2000:

TRIAL BALANCE OF R. RYAN Y/E 30 JUNE 2000

	Debit €	Credit €
Opening stock	2,700	
Purchases	40,000	
Purchases returns		1,200
Sales		86,000
Sales returns	4,900	
Repairs	490	
Discount allowed	280	
Discount received		480
Rent received		4,000
Bank charges and interest	440	
Debtors	17,000	
Creditors		14,000
Carriage in	440	
Carriage out	200	
Machinery	18,000	
Premises	80,000	
Motor vehicles	20,000	
Drawings	450	
Bank	14,000	
Cash	220	
Insurance	1,700	
Wages and salaries	3,000	
Commission	400	
Bad debts	490	
Capital		99,030
	€204,710	€204,710

Closing stock at 30 June 2000 is valued at €4,400.

EXERCISE 3

From the following Trial Balance of S. Hickey, prepare a Trading, Profit and Loss Account and Balance Sheet as at 30 September 1999.

TRIAL BALANCE OF S. HICKEY Y/E 30 SEPTEMBER 1999

	Debit €	Credit €
Purchases	38,000	
Sales		54,000
Purchases returns		800
Sales returns	520	
Opening stock	3,850	
Discount allowed	820	
Discount received		400
Bank charges	800	
Rent and rates	1,650	
Insurance	430	
Wages and salaries	10,000	
Carriage in	400	
Carriage out	830	
Debtors and Creditors	13,000	11,500
Machinery	40,000	
Premises	86,000	
Bank		2,200
Cash	450	
Drawings	810	
Bad debts	420	
Capital		129,080
	€197,980	€197,980

Closing stock is valued at €2,000.

CHAPTER 4

Fixed Assets and Depreciation

Before going on to explain the meaning of depreciation, it is necessary to distinguish between capital and revenue expenditure.

Capital expenditure is money spent on the purchase of fixed assets, e.g. plant, machinery, vehicles, furniture, premises, etc. Fixed assets are assets used by the business itself which are not for resale. They are bought by the business with a view to generating future profits and will normally last for a number of years. The value of the fixed assets is shown in the Balance Sheet as we saw in Chapter 3. The cost of these fixed assets is not treated as an expense in the Profit and Loss Account. The double-entry to record the purchase of fixed assets is:

Debit Fixed asset account, e.g. Machinery

Credit Bank account or Creditors (if the item is not yet paid for)

Revenue expenditure represents the cost of running the business on a day-to-day basis. It is all the expenditure of a business other than capital expenditure. Examples of revenue expenditure are rent, rates, wages and electricity. All such expenditure goes into the Profit and Loss Account of the business, whereas capital expenditure goes into the Balance Sheet.

The double-entry in relation to expenditure of a revenue nature is:

Debit Expense account e.g. Wages

Credit Bank account

As we saw in the previous chapter, this expense account is transferred to the Profit and Loss Account.

We need to make the distinction between revenue expenditure and capital expenditure because revenue expenditure goes into the Profit and Loss Account and capital expenditure goes into the Balance Sheet. To charge either incorrectly will result in an overstatement or understatement of the profit or loss.

It is extremely important that you can make this distinction. Confusion may arise where an item of expenditure may be revenue for one business and capital for another. For example, the purchase of a typewriter by a shoe retailer would be classified as capital expenditure. However, in a business retailing office machinery, the purchase of a typewriter would be classified as revenue as the typewriter would be stock for resale.

Depreciation

As we have already seen, fixed assets are purchased by a business for long-term use. Let us consider an example. A business purchases a machine for use at a cost of €20,000. This machine will last, say, 10 years. Rather than charging the full €20,000 to profits in the year of purchase, the business will spread the cost of this machine over its expected useful life of 10 years. In this way, the cost of the machine will be spread over 10 years rather than just the first year. After all, the business will acquire the benefit of the machine for 10 years, not just one year! Thus the profit of the first year will not be understated. In this example, the business will charge €2,000 to profits each year for 10 years in the form of depreciation and so the cost of the machine will be written off over 10 years. Depreciation simply means the writing off of an asset over its expected useful life.

Another way to view this point is that fixed assets have a limited useful life. While they are being used by the business they will fall in value every year due to wear and tear and obsolescence. Depreciation attempts to measure this and charge it against profits. To return to our example, we may assume that the machine falls in value by €2,000 each year so that after one year of use, it is no longer worth €20,000 but €18,000. At the end of year two, its value will be €16,000 and so on.

More formally, depreciation has been defined as a _measure of wearing out, consumption or other reduction in the useful economic life of a fixed asset whether arising from use, lapse of time or obsolescence through technology and market changes._

In essence, depreciation involves allocating the cost of the asset, less any residual value, over its useful life. In order to calculate the depreciation charge for a particular fixed asset, the following factors must be determined:

Cost: the cost of an asset will include all amounts necessary in order to bring the asset to a state ready for use. This normally means the purchase price of the asset plus carriage and installation charges.

Useful life: the useful life of the asset will have to be estimated, i.e. how long the fixed asset will last in the business. This can generally be determined with reasonable accuracy. For example, a computer may have a useful life of 5 years, furniture may have a useful life of 15 years and premises may have a useful life of 50 years.

Residual value: this is commonly called the scrap value of the fixed asset. This may be difficult to estimate in practice. It is the amount that the business hopes to receive for the asset when its useful life is over. For some assets, the scrap value may be zero.

EXAMPLE

A business purchases office equipment on 1 January 1999 for €40,000. It is estimated that the equipment will last for 10 years and have a residual value of €3,000 after this time.

Cost of asset	€40,000
Less residual value	(€3,000)
= amount to be depreciated	€37,000

The equipment will last for 10 years, therefore €37,000 must be divided by 10 years. €3,700 depreciation each year will be charged against profits.

Depreciation charge for 1999 =   €3,700
Depreciation charge for 2000 =   €3,700, etc.

Methods of Depreciation

There are two main methods of depreciation, namely the straight-line method and the reducing balance method.

Straight-line method: this simply charges to profit the same amount of depreciation each year. It is usually expressed as a percentage of cost.

EXAMPLE

A motor vehicle was purchased on 1 January 1998 for €15,000. It is estimated that its useful life is 5 years with nil residual value. Therefore we must spread €15,000 over 5 years and so €3,000 will be charged as depreciation each year. At the end of 1998, €3,000 will be written off the vehicle. The vehicle will then be worth €12,000.

At the end of 1999, another €3,000 will be written off the vehicle and it will then be worth €9,000. At the end of 5 years, the vehicle will be totally depreciated and its value in the Balance Sheet will then be zero.

The usual method of referring to the straight-line method in an examination paper is as in this example:

Cost of fixed asset: €15,000

Depreciation is 20% of cost (meaning 20% straight-line).

Here you would apply 20% of €15,000 each year as the depreciation charge.

Reducing balance method: some assets do not depreciate or fall in value by the same amount each year. For example, motor vehicles fall more in value in earlier years than they do in later years. For such assets it is inappropriate to use a straight-line method of depreciation, as it would not reflect the real fall in value. The reducing balance method may be more suitable. It means that the depreciation is calculated as a percentage of **net book value** each year. Net book value is the cost of the asset less depreciation already charged.

EXAMPLE

A motor vehicle was purchased on 1 January 1996 for €25,000. Depreciation is 20% per annum reducing balance.

Cost 1 January 1996	€25,000
Depreciation 1996 @ 20% of €25,000	(€5,000)
Net book value at 31/12/96	€20,000
Depreciation 1997 @ 20% of €20,000	(€4,000)
Net book value at 31/12/97	€16,000
Depreciation 1998 @ 20% of €16,000	(€3,200)
Net book value at 31/12/98	€12,800
Depreciation 1999 @ 20% of €12,800	(€2,560)
Net book value at 31/12/99	€10,240

As you can see, depreciation is calculated as a percentage of net book value, not cost. A different amount of depreciation is being charged each year, higher amounts in earlier years.

Comparison of the Two Methods

In the straight-line method, equal amounts of depreciation are charged each year. This is appropriate where assets tend to lose their value evenly throughout their life. The advantage of the straight-line method is that it is simple to operate.

In the reducing balance method, higher amounts of depreciation are charged in earlier years and lower amounts in later years. This would be appropriate where assets fall in value in that manner, e.g. motor vehicles. The advantage is that it may be more realistic for these types of assets, but it has the drawback of being more difficult to operate.

PRACTICAL COMPARISON OF BOTH METHODS

Assume a motor vehicle was purchased for €12,000 on 1 January 1994. Depreciation is applied:

1) 20% straight-line
2) 20% reducing balance.

1. 20% Straight-line

Cost 1 January 1994	€12,000
Depreciation 1994 @ 20%	(€2,400)
NBV at 31/12/94	€9,600
Depreciation 1995 @ 20%	(€2,400)
NBV at 31/12/95€7,200	€7,200
Depreciation 1996 @ 20%	(€2,400)
NBV at 31/12/96	€4,800
Depreciation 1997 @ 20%	(€2,400)
NBV at 31/12/97	€2,400
Depreciation 1998 @ 20%	(€2,400)
NBV at 31/12/98	nil

2. 20% Reducing balance

Cost 1 January 1994	€12,000
Depreciation 1994 @ 20%	(€2,400)
NBV at 31/12/94	€9,600
Depreciation 1995 @ 20% of NBV	(€1,920)
NBV at 31/12/95	€7,680
Depreciation 1996 @ 20% of NBV	(€1,536)
NBV at 31/12/96	€6,144
Depreciation 1997 @ 20% of NBV	(€1,228.80)
NBV at 31/12/97	€4,915.20
Depreciation 1998 @ 20% of NBV	(€983.04)
NBV at 31/12/98	€3,932.16

We can now see that the reducing balance method gives a different charge to depreciation from the straight-line method. The straight-line method reduces the net book value of the asset to nil. It has been totally depreciated. The reducing balance method reduces the net book value of the asset to €3,932.16. A feature of the reducing balance method is that the asset will never reach a net book value of nil, no matter how many years it is depreciated. This may be regarded as a drawback.

Accounting for Depreciation

The annual depreciation of an asset is charged against profit for the year, i.e. it is an expense in the Profit and Loss Account. You may think that the double-entry would be to debit the depreciation expense account and to credit the fixed asset account. This would be incorrect from the accounting point of view because valuable information about the original cost of the fixed asset would be lost. It is a legal requirement that companies must disclose separately in their Balance Sheets the original cost of all fixed assets and the related depreciation to date. To accomplish this, an accumulated depreciation account is opened which records the depreciation of fixed assets year after year.

Let us go through an example.

PRACTICE EXAMPLE 1

On 1 January 1997, a business purchases furniture for €16,000. Depreciation is 10% straight-line with no residual value.

To record the purchase of furniture the double-entry is:

Debit Furniture account

Credit Bank account

FURNITURE ACCOUNT

Debit					Credit
Jan. 1	Bank	16,000			

BANK ACCOUNT

Debit					Credit
			Jan. 1	Furniture	16,000

Depreciation for the year ending 31 December 1997 is 10% of €16,000 which is €1,600. The double-entry to record this depreciation is:

Debit Depreciation expense account

Credit Accumulated depreciation account

DEPRECIATION EXPENSE ACCOUNT

Debit					Credit
Dec. 31	Accumulated depreciation	1,600			

ACCUMULATED DEPRECIATION ACCOUNT

Debit					Credit
			Dec. 31	Depreciation	1,600

In this way the Fixed asset account (the furniture account) still states the original cost, €16,000, which will be incorporated into the Balance Sheet. At the end of 1997 the Depreciation expense account is transferred to the Profit and Loss Account as an expense. The double-entry for this is:

Debit Profit and Loss Account

Credit Depreciation expense account

DEPRECIATION EXPENSE ACCOUNT

Debit					Credit
Dec. 31	Accumulated depreciation	1,600	Dec. 31	Profit and Loss	1,600

PROFIT AND LOSS ACCOUNT Y/E 31 DECEMBER 1997

	Debit	Credit
	€	€
Depreciation (furniture)	1,600	

The Accumulated depreciation account is balanced at the end of 1997.

ACCUMULATED DEPRECIATION ACCOUNT

Debit					Credit
Dec. 31	Balance c/d	1,600	Dec. 31	Depreciation	1,600
			Jan. 1 1998	Balance b/d	1,600

After one year we can see that the furniture cost of €16,000 has been depreciated by €1,600, giving a net book value of €14,400. This information will appear in the Balance Sheet as follows:

BALANCE SHEET Y/E 31 DECEMBER 1997

FIXED ASSETS	COST	ACC. DEPRECIATION	NBV
Furniture	€16,000	€1,600	€14,400

Let us now continue the accounts for 1998, assuming the furniture is depreciated by another 10%.

FURNITURE ACCOUNT

Debit						Credit
Jan. 1 1997	Bank	16,000	Dec. 31 1997	Balance c/d	16,000
Jan. 1 1998	Balance b/d	16,000	Dec. 31 1998	Balance c/d	16,000
Jan. 1 1999	Balance b/d	16,000			

DEPRECIATION EXPENSE ACCOUNT

Debit					Credit
Dec. 31 1998	Accumulated depreciation	1,600	Dec. 31 1998	Profit and Loss	1,600

PROFIT AND LOSS ACCOUNT Y/E 31 DECEMBER 1998

	Debit	Credit
	€	€
Depreciation (furniture)	1,600	

ACCUMULATED DEPRECIATION ACCOUNT

Debit					Credit
Dec. 31 1997	Balance c/d	1,600	Dec. 31 1997	Depreciation	1,600
			Jan. 1 1998	Balance b/d	1,600
Dec. 31 1998	Balance c/d	3,200	Dec. 31 1998	Depreciation	1,600
		3,200			3,200
			Jan. 1 1999	Balance b/d	3,200

BALANCE SHEET Y/E 31 DECEMBER 1994

FIXED ASSETS	COST	ACC. DEPRECIATION	NBV
	€	€	€
Furniture	16,000	3,200	12,800

We can clearly see how annual depreciation goes onto the debit side of the Profit and Loss Account as it is an expense. The Balance Sheet records the original cost of the asset and the accumulated depreciation to date to arrive at the net book value (NBV). Remember, the net book value is the value of the fixed asset which has not yet been depreciated. The Accumulated depreciation account records, year after year, the annual depreciation of the fixed asset. The balance on the account will always be a credit balance which goes into the Balance Sheet under the heading 'Accumulated depreciation'.

PRACTICE EXAMPLE 2

A business purchases a motor vehicle for €14,000 on 1 January 1995. Depreciation is 20% straight-line. Prepare the ledger accounts for 1995, 1996 and 1997 including the entries in the Profit and Loss Account and Balance Sheet.

MOTOR VEHICLE ACCOUNT

Debit					Credit
Jan. 1 1995	Bank	14,000	Dec. 31 1995	Balance c/d	14,000
Jan. 1 1996	Balance b/d	14,000	Dec. 31 1996	Balance c/d	14,000
Jan. 1 1997	Balance b/d	14,000	Dec. 31 1997	Balance c/d	14,000
Jan. 1 1998	Balance b/d	14,000			

DEPRECIATION EXPENSE ACCOUNT

Debit					Credit
Dec. 31 1995	Accumulated depreciation	2,800	Dec. 31 1995	Profit and Loss	2,800
Dec. 31 1996	Accumulated depreciation	2,800	Dec. 31 1996	Profit and Loss	2,800
Dec. 31 1997	Accumulated depreciation	2,800	Dec. 31 1997	Profit and Loss	2,800

ACCUMULATED DEPRECIATION ACCOUNT

Debit					Credit
Dec. 31 1995	Balance c/d	2,800	Dec. 31 1995	Depreciation	2,800
			Jan. 1 1992	Balance b/d	2,800
Dec. 31 1996	Balance c/d	5,600	Dec. 31 1996	Depreciation	2,800
		5,600			5,600
			Jan. 1 1997	Balance b/d	5,600
Dec. 31 1997	Balance c/d	8,400	Dec. 31 1997	Depreciation	2,800
		8,400			8,400
			Jan. 1 1998	Balance b/d	8,400

PROFIT AND LOSS ACCOUNT Y/E 31 DECEMBER 1995

	Debit €	Credit €
Depreciation (motor vehicle)	2,800	

BALANCE SHEET Y/E 31 DECEMBER 1995

FIXED ASSETS	COST	ACC. DEPRECIATION	NBV
	€	€	€
Motor vehicle	14,000	2,800	11,200

PROFIT AND LOSS ACCOUNT Y/E 31 DECEMBER 1996

	Debit	Credit
	€	€
Depreciation (Motor vehicle)	2,800	

BALANCE SHEET Y/E 31 DECEMBER 1996

FIXED ASSETS	COST	ACC. DEPRECIATION	NBV
	€	€	€
Motor vehicle	14,000	5,600	8,400

PROFIT AND LOSS ACCOUNT Y/E 31 DECEMBER 1997

	Debit	Credit
	€	€
Depreciation (Motor vehicle)	2,800	

BALANCE SHEET Y/E 31 DECEMBER 1997

FIXED ASSETS	COST	ACC. DEPRECIATION	NBV
	€	€	€
Motor vehicle	14,000	8,400	5,600

We can see that the annual depreciation of €2,800 is debited to the Depreciation expense account and credited to the Accumulated depreciation account. At the end of each year, the Depreciation expense account is transferred to the Profit and Loss Account. In this way, the profits of the business are reduced to allow for the use and wear and tear of the fixed asset. The cost of the fixed asset is being written off against profits over its expected useful life.

The annual depreciation is accumulated in the Accumulated depreciation account and a balance is brought down on the credit side at the end of each year. This credit balance appears in the Balance Sheet under the heading 'Accumulated depreciation'.

The Fixed asset account for the motor vehicle remains untouched - no depreciation is entered in this account. It is balanced, of course, at the end of each year. If the business purchased vehicles or sold any, the entries would appear in the Fixed asset account.

The credit balance on the Accumulated depreciation account is deducted from the debit balance on the Motor vehicle account to arrive at the net book value of the asset. This information is recorded in the Balance Sheet.

If we continued the ledger accounts for the example for another two years, the motor vehicle would be fully depreciated and its net book value in the Balance Sheet would be nil. This means that the vehicle would be fully depreciated i.e. its cost of €14,000 would be written off against profits over 5 years. This is what depreciation aims to do: write the cost of a fixed asset over its expected useful life.

PRACTICE EXAMPLE 3

A business purchased a motor vehicle for €12,000 on 1 January 1996. Its accounting year ends on 31 December. Depreciation is charged at 20% reducing balance. Show the ledger accounts for the first two years, and the entries in the Profit and Loss Account and Balance Sheet.

PRACTICE EXAMPLE 3 SOLUTION

MOTOR VEHICLES ACCOUNT

Debit					Credit
Jan. 1 1996	Bank	12,000	Dec. 31 1996	Balance c/d	12,000
Jan. 1 1997	Balance b/d	12,000	Dec. 31 1997	Balance c/d	12,000
Jan. 1 1998	Balance b/d	12,000			

ACCUMULATED DEPRECIATION ACCOUNT MOTOR VEHICLES

Debit					Credit
Dec. 31 1996	Balance c/d	2,400	Dec. 31 1996	Depreciation	2,400
			Jan. 1 1997	Balance b/d	2,400
Dec. 31 1997	Balance c/d	4,320	Dec. 31 1997	Depreciation	1,920
		4,320			4,320
			Jan. 1 1998	Balance b/d	4,320

DEPRECIATION EXPENSE ACCOUNT

Debit					Credit
Dec. 31 1996	Acc. depreciation	2,400	Dec. 31 1996	Profit and Loss	2,400
Dec. 31 1997	Acc. depreciation	1,920	Dec. 31 1997	Profit and Loss	1,920

PROFIT AND LOSS ACCOUNT Y/E 31 DECEMBER 1996

	Debit €	Credit €
Depreciation motor vehicles	2,400	

BALANCE SHEET Y/E 31 DECEMBER 1996

FIXED ASSETS	COST €	ACC. DEPRECIATION €	NBV €
Motor vehicles	12,000	2,400	9,600

PROFIT AND LOSS ACCOUNT Y/E 31 DECEMBER 1997

	Debit €	Credit €
Depreciation motor vehicles	1,920	

BALANCE SHEET Y/E 31 DECEMBER 1997

FIXED ASSETS	COST	ACC. DEPRECIATION	NBV
	€	€	€
Motor vehicles	12,000	4,320	7,680

NOTE:

Cost of motor vehicle, 1 Jan. 1996	€12,000
Depreciation 1996, 20%	(€2,400)
Net book value at 31/12/96	€9,600
Depreciation 1997, 20%	(€1,920)
Net book value at 31/12/97	€7,680

PRACTICE EXAMPLE 4

The following is an extract from the Trial Balance of a business at 1 January 1999:

	Debit	Credit
	€	€
Motor vehicles - cost	30,000	
Accumulated depreciation - motor vehicles		10,800
Premises - cost	70,000	
Accumulated depreciation - premises		12,400
Machinery - cost	14,000	
Accumulated depreciation - machinery		1,400

Depreciation is calculated as follows:

Motor vehicles - 20% p.a. reducing balance

Premises - 5% p.a. straight-line

Machinery - 10% p.a. straight-line

Show the Profit and Loss Account and Balance Sheet entries for the year ending 31 December 1999.

PRACTICE EXAMPLE 4 SOLUTION

Depreciation of motor vehicles @ 20% p.a. reducing balance:

Cost of motor vehicles	€30,000
Accumulated depreciation to date	(€10,800)
= NBV at 1/1/99	€19,200
Depreciation for 1999 = 20% x €19,200	(€3,840)
= NBV at 31/12/99	€15,360
Depreciation of premises @ 5% p.a. straight-line:	
Cost of premises	€70,000
Depreciation for 1999 = 5% x 70,000	(3,500)

In order to calculate the net book value for Balance Sheet purposes, the accumulated depreciation to date in the Trial Balance must be added to the 1999 depreciation and the total subtracted from the original value of the premises i.e. 70,000 - (12,400 + 3,500) = €54,100.

Depreciation of machinery 10% p.a. straight-line:

Cost of machinery	€14,000
Depreciation for 1999 @ 10%	(1,400)

NBV for machinery will be calculated in the same manner as for premises.

PROFIT AND LOSS ACCOUNT Y/E 31 DECEMBER 1999

	Debit	Credit
	€	€
Depreciation motor vehicles	3,840	
Depreciation premises	3,500	
Depreciation machinery	1,400	

BALANCE SHEET Y/E 31 DECEMBER 1999

FIXED ASSETS	COST	ACC. DEPRECIATION	NBV
	€	€	€
Motor vehicles	30,000	14,640	15,360
Premises	70,000	15,900	54,100
Machinery	14,000	2,800	11,200

We can see from the Trial Balance that the original cost of all Fixed assets is in the debit column. What appears in the credit column under 'Accumulated depreciation' is the total depreciation written off each respective asset to date. This figure will be the opening credit balance in the Accumulated depreciation account. The depreciation for this year is added to this opening balance to find the closing credit balance in the Accumulated depreciation account which is entered in the Balance Sheet.

In order to see where these figures came from, let us do the ledger accounts.

MOTOR VEHICLES ACCOUNT

Debit						Credit
Jan. 1 2000	Balance b/d	30,000				

ACCUMULATED DEPRECIATION ACCOUNT MOTOR VEHICLES

Debit						Credit
			Jan. 1 1999	Balance b/d	10,800
Dec. 31 1999	Balance c/d	14,640	Dec. 31 1999	Depreciation	3,840
		14,640			14,640
			Jan. 1 2000	Balance b/d	14,640

PREMISES ACCOUNT

Debit					Credit
Jan. 1 2000	Balance b/d	70,000			

ACCUMULATED DEPRECIATION ACCOUNT PREMISES

Debit					Credit
			Jan. 1 1999	Balance b/d	12,400
Dec. 31 1999	Balance c/d	15,900	Dec. 31 1999	Depreciation	3,500
		15,900			15,900
			Jan. 1 2000	Balance b/d	15,900

MACHINERY ACCOUNT

Debit					Credit
Jan. 1 1999	Balance b/d	14,000			

ACCUMULATED DEPRECIATION ACCOUNT MACHINERY

Debit					Credit
			Jan. 1 1999	Balance b/d	1,400
Dec. 31 1999	Balance c/d	2,800	Dec. 31 1999	Depreciation	1,400
		2,800			2,800
			Jan. 1 2000	Balance b/d	2,800

EXERCISE 1

A business purchased two fixed assets for cash on 1 January 1999. These were:

1. 20 year lease on a Premises costing €80,000
2. Motor vehicle costing €14,000 which has an estimated useful life of 5 years and a residual value of €1,500.

Calculate the annual depreciation charge on the above assets.

Assuming accounts end on 31 December, show the ledger accounts, Profit and Loss Account and Balance Sheet entries for y/e 31 December 1999.

EXERCISE 2

On 1 January 1998 a business has in its books a motor vehicle at a cost of €10,000, accumulated depreciation, €3,600. It also has furniture at a cost of €12,000, accumulated depreciation €3,600. Depreciation of motor vehicles is 20% p.a. reducing balance. Depreciation of furniture is 10% p.a. straight-line.

Show the ledger accounts, Profit and Loss Account and Balance Sheet entries for y/e 31 December 1998.

EXERCISE 3

Identify four factors which cause fixed assets to depreciate.

Which of the four factors is the most important for each of the following fixed assets?

1. A 90 year lease on a building.
2. Land.
3. A forest of mature trees to be felled for timber.
4. A computer after the launch of an improved model capable of increased efficiency and quality.

CHAPTER 5

Accruals and Prepayments

Final Accounts are usually prepared for a definite accounting period, say one year. So far when preparing our Final Accounts in Chapter 3 we have assumed that expenses relate to the period in which they are paid and so there are no prepayments or accruals. Similar assumptions have been made regarding income. In practice, however, if we take the expenses paid or income received by a business, it is most unlikely that they will exactly match the accounting period. It is almost certain that some expenses, such as electricity, telephone, etc., which are due in the accounting year will not have been paid at the end of it. An adjustment in the Final Accounts will need to be made for these accruals. Other business expenses, such as insurance, rent, rates, etc., may be overpaid in the accounting year. A prepayment exists at the end of the year and again must be adjusted for.

In the ledger accounts, the expense accounts will record the amounts that have been paid by cheque or cash during the accounting year - they will not make an allowance for accruals and prepayments. It is a concept of accounting, called the **accruals concept**, that when preparing the Profit and Loss Account, expenses charged to profit relate to the full accounting period, whether or not they have actually been paid. In other words, the expenses that relate to the year go into the Profit and Loss Account, not necessarily the amount that was paid. For example, the Profit and Loss Account should charge one full year's rent, rates, wages, electricity, etc.

The same principle applies to income in the Profit and Loss Account i.e. the income that goes into the Profit and Loss Account is the income that relates to the year, not necessarily what was actually received.

In examination questions these adjustments for accruals and prepayments are usually shown as notes at the end of the Trial Balance.

Accruals

An accrual is an amount owed by a business at the end of the accounting period. It is therefore a liability to the business. The amount owing at the end of the year appears as a credit balance brought down in the appropriate ledger account.

PRACTICE EXAMPLE 1

A business has to pay rent from 1 January to 31 December 2000 of €1,000. The rent is paid every quarter on 1 January, 1 April, 1 July and 1 October, being €250 per quarter. Assume that the €250 due on 1 October is not paid in 2000. The Rent account will appear as follows:

RENT ACCOUNT

Debit					Credit
Jan. 1	Bank	250			
Apr. 1	Bank	250			
July 1	Bank	250			

The business paid €750 rent on the above dates, so the double-entry is:

Debit Rent account €750

Credit Bank account €750

We know that a further €250 is due in respect of 2000 and this accrual has to be shown as a credit balance b/d in the Rent account to represent a liability. At the end of 2000, a full year's rent has to be transferred to the Profit and Loss Account. To do this, the entry is:

Debit Profit and Loss Account €1,000

Credit Rent account €1,000

So the complete Rent account appears as follows:

RENT ACCOUNT

Debit					Credit
Jan. 1	Bank	250			
Apr. 1	Bank	250			
July 1	Bank	250			
Dec. 31 2000	Balance c/d	250	Dec. 31 2000	Profit and Loss	1,000
		1,000			1,000
			Jan. 1 2001	Balance b/d	250

The €250 closing balance will be shown in the Balance Sheet as at 31 December 2000 as a current liability - accrued rent.

As we can see from this example, the rent figure that appears in the Profit and Loss Account at 31 December 2000 is €1,000, not €750. Again it must be stressed what goes into the Profit and Loss Account is the _total_ expense for the year, regardless of what has been paid.

PRACTICE EXAMPLE 2

A business is charged €2,500 for rates for 2000. The amount actually paid during the year is €2,350. The Rates account is as follows:

RATES ACCOUNT

Debit					Credit
2000	Bank	2,350			
Dec. 31 2000	Balance c/d	150	Dec. 31 2000	Profit and Loss	2,500
		2,500			2,500
			Jan. 1 2001	Balance b/d	150

To record the payment of rates:

Debit Rates account €2,350

Credit Bank account €2,350

We see that €150 is still owed in rates for 2000. This is shown as a credit balance brought down, representing a current liability in the Balance Sheet. The total expense for rates charged to the Profit and Loss Account for 2000 is €2,500. The entry to record this is :

Debit Profit and Loss Account €2,500

Credit Rates account €2,500

The entries in the Profit and Loss Account and Balance Sheet for the year ending 31 December 2000 are as follows:

PROFIT AND LOSS ACCOUNT Y/E 31 DECEMBER 2000

	Debit	Credit
	€	€
Rates	2,500	
(paid €2,350, add due €150)		

BALANCE SHEET Y/E 31 DECEMBER 2000

CURRENT LIABILITIES	€
Rates due	150

You can see that all expense ledger accounts are closed off at the end of the year and transferred to the Profit and Loss Account. The same applied in Chapter 4 in relation to the Depreciation expense account which was transferred to the Profit and Loss Account. This explains what we saw in Chapter 1 - how we did not actually 'balance' these accounts. Of course, if there is an accrual or prepayment in the ledger accounts, the accrual or prepayment is shown as a balance b/d which goes into the Balance Sheet. All accruals and prepayments are dealt with twice in the accounts - once in the Profit and Loss Account and once again in the Balance Sheet.

Prepayments

Certain expenses of a business may be paid in advance, that is, some of the expense paid relates to the next accounting year. These prepaid amounts are assets to the business and must therefore appear as debit balances brought down in the ledger accounts.

PRACTICE EXAMPLE 3

Assume a business has an expense for insurance of €800 for 2000. The amount paid was actually €900. The Insurance account will appear as follows:

INSURANCE ACCOUNT

Debit					Credit
2000	Bank	900			

The business paid €900 insurance, so the double-entry is:

Debit Insurance account €900

Credit Bank account €900

However, €100 of this payment does not relate to 2000 but to next year so there is a prepayment of €100. This €100 has to be shown as a debit balance b/d in the Insurance account representing an asset to the business. At the end of 2000, only this year's expense of insurance is transferred to the Profit and Loss Account, i.e. €800. To do this, the double-entry is:

Debit Profit and Loss Account €800

Credit Insurance account €800

So the complete Insurance account is as follows:

INSURANCE ACCOUNT

Debit					Credit
2000	Bank	900	Dec. 31 2000	Profit and Loss	800
			Dec. 31 2000	Balance c/d	100
		900			900
Jan. 1 2001	Balance b/d	100			

The €100 closing balance will appear in the Balance Sheet for the year ending 31 December 2000 as a current asset of prepaid insurance. As we can see, the insurance figure that goes into the Profit and Loss Account is €800, not €900. Again, what goes into the Profit and Loss Account is the expense that relates to the period, regardless of what has been paid.

PRACTICE EXAMPLE 4

Rates of €1,250 are paid by a business in an accounting year running from 1 January to 31 December 2000. This payment of €1,250 relates to the period of 15 months from 1 January to 31 March 2001. So this amount covers 15 months and the accounting period is 12 months. Therefore, 3 months' rates have been paid in advance. Only €1,000 of the rates is an expense for 2000. The remaining €250 will become an expense in 2001. At 31 December 2000, this €250 represents a prepayment, an asset, and so there is a debit balance in the Rates account.

RATES ACCOUNT

Debit					Credit
2000	Bank	1,250	Dec. 31 2000	Profit and Loss	1,000
			Dec. 31 2000	Balance c/d	250
		1,250			1,250
Jan. 1 2001	Balance b/d	250			

The double-entry for the payment of €1,250 rates is:

Debit Rates account €1,250

Credit Bank account €1,250

The double-entry for the expense of rates for 2000:

Debit Profit and Loss Account €1,000

Credit Rates account €1,000

The entries in the Profit and Loss Account and Balance Sheet are:

PROFIT AND LOSS ACCOUNT Y/E 31 DECEMBER 2000

	Debit €	Credit €
Rates	1,000	
(paid €1,250, less prepaid €250)		

BALANCE SHEET Y/E 31 DECEMBER 2000

	€
CURRENT ASSETS	
Rates prepaid	250

Accruals of Income/Revenue

Income relating to an accounting period, but not received by the end of that period, is an asset and must therefore appear as a debit balance b/d in the ledger account. It is similar to debtors - the business is owed money.

PRACTICE EXAMPLE 5

Rent is received in an accounting year 1 January to 31 December 2000 amounting to €600.
The actual amount of rent that should have been received is €700. This means that we are still
owed €100 in rent for 2000.

RENT RECEIVABLE ACCOUNT (Income account)

Debit					Credit
Dec. 31 2000	Profit and Loss	700	2000 Dec. 31 2000	Bank Balance c/d	600 100
		700			700
Jan. 1 2001	Balance b/d	100			

To record the €600 rent received, the double-entry is:

Debit Bank account €600

Credit Rent receivable account €600

The amount transferred to the Profit and Loss Account for the year ending 31 December 2000
is €700, representing income *earned* in 2000. The double-entry is:

Debit Rent receivable account €700

Credit Profit and Loss Account €700

The €100 closing balance is shown in the Balance Sheet at 31 December 2000 as a current asset.

The entries in the Profit and Loss Account and Balance Sheet are:

PROFIT AND LOSS ACCOUNT Y/E 31 DECEMBER 2000

	Debit €	Credit €
Rent receivable		700
(received €600, add due €100)		

BALANCE SHEET Y/E 31 DECEMBER 2000

CURRENT ASSETS	€
Rent receivable due	100

Prepayment of Income/Revenue

A prepayment of income, that is an overpayment of income actually due, represents a liability
and must therefore appear as a credit balance brought down in the ledger account.

PRACTICE EXAMPLE 6

Rent is received in an accounting year 1 January to 31 December 2000 of €2,500 covering the period
1 January 2000 to 31 March 2001. This shows that 15 months' rent has been received in a 12 month
accounting period. Therefore, 3 months' rent is overpaid, i.e. €500.

RENT RECEIVABLE ACCOUNT

Debit					Credit
Dec. 31 2000	Profit and Loss	2,000	2000	Bank	2,500
Dec. 31 2000	Balance c/d	500			
		2,500			2,500
			Jan. 1 2001	Balance b/d	500

To record the €2,500 rent received, the double-entry is:

Debit Bank account €2,500

Credit Rent received account €2,500

Only €2,000 is transferred to the Profit and Loss Account at 31 December 2000, representing the income _earned_ in 2000. The double-entry is:

Debit Rent receivable account €2,000

Credit Profit and Loss Account €2,000

The €500 closing balance is shown in the Balance Sheet year ending 31 December 2000 as a current liability.

The entries in the Profit and Loss Account and Balance Sheet are;

PROFIT AND LOSS ACCOUNT Y/E 31 DECEMBER 2000

	Debit	Credit
	€	€
Rent receivable		2,000
(received €2,500, less prepaid		
€500)		

BALANCE SHEET Y/E 31 DECEMBER 2000

CURRENT LIABILITIES	€
Rent receivable prepaid	500

The entries in the Final Accounts to provide for accruals and prepayments will present no problem if we remember to charge to the Profit and Loss Account the correct expenditure relating to that period only and to credit it with the correct income. This means that we must exclude income or expenditure which is included in the accounts but relates to the past period or the next one. You must remember the following:

Expenses due by a business (accruals) at the end of an accounting period are _added_ to the appropriate expense paid in the Profit and Loss Account. This is because the accrued expense applies to that accounting period even though it is not yet actually paid. The accrual is also entered in the Balance Sheet as a current liability as it is now a debt due and will be paid within the year.

Income owing to a business (accruals of income) at the end of an accounting period is also_added_ to the appropriate receipt in the Profit and Loss Account, because it constitutes income for the actual period which has not, as yet, been actually received. The receipt due is also entered in the Balance Sheet as a current asset.

Prepayments of expenses made by a business are payments made in the present accounting period which relate to next year. The amount is _deducted_ from the appropriate expense paid in the Profit and Loss Account. It is entered in the Balance Sheet as a current asset.

Prepayments of income made to a business are received in the present accounting period but relate to next year. These are _deducted_ from the appropriate income received in the Profit and Loss Account and are entered in the Balance Sheet as a current liability.

These adjustments are stated as notes to the Trial Balance in examination questions. For example:

TRIAL BALANCE AS AT 31 DECEMBER

	Debit	Credit
	€	€
Insurance	500	
Wages	1,200	

NOTES:

Insurance prepaid €100

Wages due €500

The amounts in the Trial Balance represent the amount paid for these expenses.

1. Insurance: €500 was paid for the year, but out of this €100 was prepaid. The charge or actual expense of insurance is €400. The charge to the Profit and Loss Account is €400 and €100 appears as a current asset in the Balance Sheet.

2. Wages: €1,200 was paid for the year but €500 is still owing. The charge or actual expense of wages for the year is €1,700 in the Profit and Loss Account. €500 appears as a current liability in the Balance Sheet.

EXERCISE 1

During 2000, the following payments were made relating to rent:

Jan. 1: €900 for 1 January to 31 March.
Mar. 15: €900 for 1 April to 30 June.
July 8: €900 for 1 July to 30 September.

The accounting year runs from 1 January to 31 December 2000. Prepare the Rent account for 2000. Show the entries in the Profit and Loss Account and Balance Sheet for the year of 2000.

EXERCISE 2

A trader pays insurance in 2000 as follows:

Jan. 1: €400 for 1 January to 30 June.
June 28: €400 for 1 July to 31 December.
Dec. 12: €400 for 1 January to 30 June 2001.

The accounting year runs from 1 January to 31 December 2000. Prepare the Insurance account for 2000. Show the entries in the Profit and Loss Account and Balance Sheet for the year ending 31 December 2000.

EXERCISE 3

A trader rents a property to a tenant on 1 January 2000 at an agreed rental of €10,000 per annum. The following cash receipts occur:

Jan. 1 2000: €2,500
Apr. 1 2000: €2,500
July 8 2000: €2,500
Jan. 2 2000: €2,500

The accounting year runs from 1 January to 31 December 2000. Prepare the ledger account for Rent receivable and show the entries in the Profit and Loss Account and Balance Sheet for year ending 31 December 2000.

EXERCISE 4

A trader rents out property and receives rent quarterly of €300. The property was first rented on 1 March 2000 and the due dates for the receipt of rent are 31 May, 31 August, 30 November and 28 February. Rent is received on the due dates.

The accounting year runs from 1 January to 31 December 2000. Prepare the ledger account for Rent receivable and show the entries in the Profit and Loss Account and Balance Sheet for year ending 31 December 2000.

EXERCISE 5

On 1 July 1999, a trader has telephone expenses accrued of €800. The charge for telephone for the accounting period 1 July 1999 to 30 June 2000 is €4,000. Telephone expenses were paid as follows:

July 3 1999: €650
Dec. 2 1999: €1,000
Feb. 3 2000: €2,000
Apr. 1 2000: €1,500
June 1 2000: €1,500

Prepare the Telephone expenses account and show the entries in the Profit and Loss Account and Balance Sheet for year ending 30 June 2000.

EXERCISE 6

On 1 July 1999, a trader has a prepayment of rates of €400. The charge for rates for the accounting year 1 July 1999 to 30 June, 2000 is €12,000. Rates were paid as follows:

Aug. 8 1999: €490
Nov. 10 1999: €8,000
Apr. 1 2000: €2,000

Prepare the Rates account and show the entries in the Profit and Loss Account and Balance Sheet for year ending 30 June 2000.

CHAPTER 6

Bad Debts and Bad Debts Provisions

Bad Debts

When a business sells goods on credit, there is a risk that some debtors will not pay the amount due. Here the business has to bear the loss and this loss is called a **bad debt**. Well-managed businesses take care not to sell to any customer where there is a high risk of non-payment. They are also likely to have a credit control system in operation to ensure that all debts are collected within a reasonable time. Even despite this, businesses must accept that inevitably some debts will turn out to be bad debts. A bad debt is a normal business risk and it is written off to the Profit and Loss Account as an expense. The double-entry for a bad debt written off is:

Debit Bad debts account

Credit Debtors account

For example, on 1 May goods were sold on credit to Mr Hynes for €800. On 8 July Mr Hynes paid €700 and then went bankrupt. The remaining €100 owing was written off as a bad debt.

DEBTORS ACCOUNT - MR HYNES

Debit						Credit
May 1	Sales	800	July 8	Bank		700
			July 8	Bad debts		100
		800				800

BAD DEBTS ACCOUNT

Debit					Credit
July 8	Debtors: Mr Hynes	100	Dec. 31	Profit and Loss	100

The double-entry for the bad debt written off is:

Debit Bad debts account €100

Credit Debtors account (Mr Hynes) €100

This Bad debts account is an expense account and so is transferred to the Profit and Loss Account, the entry being:

Debit Profit and Loss Account €100

Credit Bad debts account €100

The occurrence of a bad debt means that what was <u>believed</u> to be, and had been treated as, an asset i.e. Debtors, is now known <u>not</u> to be an asset. Instead an expense is recognised. Therefore the double-entry for bad debts written off reflects a reduction in an asset (Debtors) and an increase in expenses (Bad debts). In the above example, the debtors figure relating to Mr Hynes will not appear in the Balance Sheet as an asset since the account is closed off. The effect will be shown in the Profit and Loss Account where the net profit will be reduced by €100 as a result of the expense of a bad debt.

Let us take another example:

John Corbett, a debtor, who owes the business €4,000 makes a settlement on 1 October 1999 to pay 90p in the €. The balance is to be written off as a bad debt. The ledger accounts are as follows:

DEBTORS ACCOUNT (JOHN CORBETT)

Debit					Credit
Jan. 1 1999	Balance b/d	4,000	Oct. 1 1999	Bank	3,600
			Oct. 1 1999	Bad debts	400
		4,000			4,000

BAD DEBTS ACCOUNT

Debit					Credit
Oct. 1 1999	Debtors	400	Dec. 31 1999	Profit and Loss	400

PROFIT AND LOSS ACCOUNT Y/E 31 DECEMBER 1999

	Debit €	Credit €
Bad debts written off	400	

The debt is not always written in full. Sometimes a debtor can make an arrangement with his creditors to pay part of the debt in a final settlement.

Bad Debts Recovered

Occasionally, where an amount due has been treated as a bad debt and written off, it may be eventually recovered and the cash received. When this occurs, the business reverses the accounting entries for bad debts written off. The amount of the bad debt recovered is recognised as income in the period in which it is received. The double-entry to record a bad debt recovered is:

Debit Bank/Cash account

Credit Bad debts recovered account

At the end of the accounting year, the Bad debts recovered account is transferred to the Profit and Loss Account where it will appear as income.

Consider the previous example. Assume John Corbett makes a payment of €400 on 12 January 2000 covering the amount that was previously written off as a bad debt in 1999. The ledger accounts are:

BANK ACCOUNT

Debit						Credit
Jan. 12 2000	Bad debt recovered	400				

BAD DEBTS RECOVERED ACCOUNT

Debit					Credit
Dec. 31 2000	Profit and Loss	400	Jan. 12 2000	Bank	400

PROFIT AND LOSS ACCOUNT Y/E 31 DECEMBER 2000

	Debit	Credit
	€	€
Bad debts recovered		400

An alternative approach to this is to reopen the debt that was written off in the debtors account. This is what would be done in practice in the debtor's personal account. The entries would be:

Debit Debtors account

Credit Bad debts recovered account

and

Debit Bank/Cash account

Credit Debtors account

As before, the Bad debts recovered account would be transferred to the Profit and Loss Account.

This makes sense. If a bad debt were recovered, the accountant for the business would firstly go to the personal file of this debtor and reopen the debt. She would then make an entry for payment received in the debtor's account. This account would be closed showing a debit and a credit entry for the bad debt recovered. The debtor in question would be pleased to know that the payment made was recorded in his personal account. But for examination purposes, we do not normally deal with the personal ledgers, only the Debtors control account. The Debtors control account is a summary of all the information in the personal ledgers relating to debtors. It is accepted that the double-entry for bad debts recovered is:

Debit Bank/Cash account

Credit Bad debts recovered account

Provision for Bad Debts

After the business has written off the debts known to be bad, it must make provisions for debts that are not yet bad but may be doubtful. At the end of each accounting period it is necessary to estimate the extent of doubtful debts. There are the debts outstanding at the end of the year that are uncertain of recovery. There may be some hope of collecting them. It is important that we do not overstate the value of debtors in the Balance Sheet by including debts that may prove to be bad i.e. the doubtful debts.

At the end of the accounting year, the manager or accountant of the business examines all the debtors and makes a list of those he or she considers from experience to be unable or unwilling to pay. The total of this list represents the probable amount of bad debts in the next accounting period.

A quicker way of estimating doubtful debts is to apply an overall percentage of the debtors figure, say, 5% of total debtors. This method may not be as accurate as going through each debtor in detail and ageing them, but in examination papers the provision for bad debts is usually calculated as a percentage of debtors.

The double-entry needed in order to create a provision for bad/doubtful debts is:

Debit Profit and Loss Account

Credit Provision for bad debts account

You should note that the amount created as a provision for bad debts does not go into the Debtors account. There is still a possibility this provision may be collected. It is only when the bad debt is written off in full that the debtors account is credited.

A provision is usually defined as *an amount set aside out of profits to provide for any known expense which cannot be determined with accuracy.* The amount of the provision created is debited to the Profit and Loss Account, thus creating an expense for the year. This is in accordance with the **prudence concept** of accounting. The prudence concept states that if a business has the possibility of suffering an expense, it should write it off against profits immediately. This is what is happening here. The business has the possibility of bad debts, so it is writing the amount off in the Profit and Loss Account and so reducing profit for the year.

PRACTICE EXAMPLE 1

A trader whose total debtors are €80,000 on 1 January 1997 estimates that 5% of these will be bad at the end of the year. He decides to make a provision in his accounts for this.

To calculate the provision:

5% of €80,000 = €4,000

This means that out of €80,000 owed, the trader estimates that €4,000 is irrecoverable. Remember, we are not writing it off as a bad debt - there is still a possibility that it might be paid. We are only setting the €4,000 aside against profits. The double-entry is:

Debit Profit and Loss Account €4,000

Credit Provision for bad debts account €4,000

DEBTORS ACCOUNT

Debit					Credit
Jan. 1 1997	Balance b/d	80,000	31 Dec. 1997	Balance c/d	80,000
Jan. 1 1998	Balance b/d	80,000			

PROVISION FOR BAD DEBTS ACCOUNT

Debit					Credit
Dec. 31 1997	Balance c/d	4,000	Dec. 31 1997	Profit and Loss	4,000
			Jan. 1 1998	Balance b/d	4,000

PROFIT AND LOSS ACCOUNT Y/E 31 DECEMBER 1997

	Debit	Credit
	€	€
Provision for bad debts	4,000	

As we can see, the debtors ledger account is untouched - it still shows €80,000 owing. There is a credit balance in the Provision for bad debts account of €4,000 and the Profit and Loss Account is debited with €4,000. The balance in the Provision for bad debts account is deducted from the debtors figure in the Balance Sheet.

BALANCE SHEET Y/E 31 DECEMBER 1997

CURRENT ASSETS	€	€
Debtors	80,000	
less provision for bad debts	(4,000)	76,000

The Balance Sheet entry shows the debtors at what we estimate their true value to be, i.e. the amount of debtors that can readily be turned into cash. In other words, the closing balance in the Provision for bad debts account (being a credit balance) is deducted from the closing balance in the debtors account (being a debit balance).

Increase/Decrease in Provision for Bad Debts

In subsequent accounting periods, bad debts continue to be written off to the bad debts account. The trader may want to change the amount set aside in his Provision for bad debts account to reflect more accurate information. He may want to increase this provision if he feels that there is not enough set aside to reflect bad debts. This may be because there is a greater amount of debtors. The double-entry to reflect an increase in the provision for bad debts is:

Debit Profit and Loss Account

Credit Provision for bad debts account

with the amount of the increase in the provision needed.

If the provision needs to be decreased, the double-entry is:

Debit Provision for bad debts account

Credit Profit and Loss Account

with the amount of decrease in the provision.

PRACTICE EXAMPLE 2

We will take the information from Practice Example 1. A trader at 1 January 1998 has debtors of €80,000 and a provision for bad debts created of €4,000. During 1998, total sales are €230,000 with payments made of €215,000. The trader wants to maintain a provision for bad debts of 5% at the endof 1998.

DEBTORS ACCOUNT

Debit						Credit
Jan. 1 1998	Balance b/d	80,000	1998	Bank		215,000
1998	Sales	230,000	Dec. 31 1998	Balance c/d		95,000
		310,000				310,000
Jan. 1 1999	Balance b/d	95,000				

PROVISION FOR BAD DEBTS ACCOUNT

Debit						Credit
			Jan. 1 1998	Balance b/d		4,000
Dec. 31 1998	Balance c/d	4,750	Dec. 31 1998	Profit and Loss		750
		4,750				4,750
			Jan. 1 1999	Balance b/d		4,750

PROFIT AND LOSS ACCOUNT Y/E 31 DECEMBER 1998

	Debit	Credit
	€	€
Increase in provision for bad debts	750	

As we can see from the above, the new provision created at 31 December 1998 is calculated as 5% of the closing debtors figure of €95,000, equalling €4,750. This suggests an increase in the provision of €750 during 1998. The double-entry is:

Debit Profit and Loss Account €750

Credit Provision for bad debts account €750

There is a credit balance on the Provision for bad debts account of €4,750 equalling 5% of €95,000. The Balance Sheet is as follows:

BALANCE SHEET Y/E 31 DECEMBER 1998

CURRENT ASSETS	€	€
Debtors	95,000	
less provision for bad debts	(4,750)	90,250

PRACTICE EXAMPLE 3

We will continue the above ledger accounts for the year 1999. During 1999, total sales are €300,000 with payments made of €350,000. The trader wants to maintain a provision for bad debts of 5% of debtors at the end of 1999.

DEBTORS ACCOUNT

Debit					Credit
Jan. 1 1999	Balance b/d	95,000	1999	Bank	350,000
1999	Sales	300,000	Dec. 31 1999	Balance c/d	45,000
		395,000			395,000
Jan. 1 2000	Balance b/d	45,000			

PROVISION FOR BAD DEBTS ACCOUNT

Debit					Credit
Dec. 31 1999	Profit and Loss	2,500	Jan. 1 1999	Balance b/d	4,750
Dec. 31 1999	Balance c/d	2,250			
		4,750			4,750
			Jan. 1 2000	Balance b/d	2,250

PROFIT AND LOSS ACCOUNT Y/E 31 DECEMBER 1999

	Debit	Credit
	€	€
Decrease in provision for bad debts		2,500

The new provision created at 31 December 1999 is calculated as 5% of €45,000 = €2,250. This suggests a decrease of €2,500 during 1999. The double-entry is:

Debit Provision for bad debts account €2,500

Credit Profit and Loss Account €2,500

The trader had too much money set aside to provide for doubtful debts. The amount of the decrease is clawed back into his profits as a credit in the Profit and Loss Account. The Balance Sheet entry is:

BALANCE SHEET Y/E 31 DECEMBER 1999

CURRENT ASSETS	€	€
Debtors	45,000	
less provision for bad debts	(2,250)	42,750

PRACTICE EXAMPLE 4

On 1 January 1997 the balance on the Provision for bad debts account of a trader was €4,000, being 5% of debtors on that date. During 1997 and 1998 bad debts written off amounted to €2,000 and €2,800 respectively. Credit sales for 1997 and 1998 were €86,000 and €98,000 respectively. Payments by debtors for 1997 and 1998 were €81,000 and €112,000 respectively. The trader wishes to maintain a provision for bad debts of 5% of debtors at the end of each year. Write up the Debtors account, Bad debts expense account and Provision for bad debts account for 1997 and 1998, and show the entries in the Profit and Loss Account and Balance Sheet for the two years.

PRACTICE EXAMPLE 4 SOLUTION

DEBTORS ACCOUNT

Debit					Credit
Jan. 1 1997	Balance b/d	80,000	1997	Bad debts	2,000
1997	Sales	86,000	1997	Bank	81,000
			Dec. 31 1997	Balance c/d	83,000
		166,000			166,000
Jan. 1 1998	Balance b/d	83,000	1998	Bad debts	2,800
1998	Sales	98,000	1998	Bank	112,000
			Dec. 31 1998	Balance c/d	66,200
		181,000			181,000
Jan. 1 1999	Balance b/d	66,200			

BAD DEBTS (EXPENSE) ACCOUNT

Debit					Credit
1997	Debtors	2,000	Dec. 1 1997	Profit and Loss	2,000
1998	Debtors	2,800	Dec. 31 1998	Profit and Loss	2,800

PROVISION FOR BAD DEBTS ACCOUNT

Debit					Credit
			Jan. 1 1997	Balance b/d	4,000
Dec. 31 1997	Balance c/d	4,150	Dec. 31 1997	Profit and Loss	150
		4,150			4,150
Dec. 31 1998	Profit and Loss	840	Jan. 1 1998	Balance b/d	4,150
Dec. 31 1998	Balance c/d	3,310			
		4,150			4,150
			Jan. 1 1999	Balance b/d	3,310

PROFIT AND LOSS ACCOUNT Y/E 31 DECEMBER 1997

	Debit	Credit
	€	€
Bad debts written off	2,000	
Increase in bad debts provision	150	

BALANCE SHEET Y/E 31 DECEMBER 1997

CURRENT ASSETS	€	€
Debtors	83,000	
less provision for bad debts	(4,150)	78,850

PROFIT AND LOSS ACCOUNT Y/E 31 DECEMBER 1998

	Debit	Credit
	€	€
Bad debts written off	2,800	
Decrease in bad debts provision		840

BALANCE SHEET Y/E 31 DECEMBER 1998

CURRENT ASSETS	€	€
Debtors	66,200	
less provision for bad debts	(3,310)	62,890

Provisions for Discounts

Some firms have a policy of allowing discounts to debtors if they pay the amounts due to the business within a specified period of time. It would be prudent for such businesses to examine the debtors at the end of the accounting period and make a provision for these discounts. This is in accordance with the accounting concept of prudence - anticipating losses and making a provision for them in the Profit and Loss Account. The accounting treatment is similar to that for the provision for bad debts:

Debit Profit and Loss Account

Credit Provision for discounts allowed account

The calculation of the provision for discounts allowed is usually made as a percentage of debtors. If a business has created a provision for bad debts and a provision for discounts allowed, the calculation of the provision for discounts is made on the net debtors. i.e. debtors less provision for bad debts. In other words, you should calculate the % provision for bad debts first using the debtors figure. Deduct the bad debts provision from the debtors figure and then calculate the % provision for discounts. No business would provide for discounts allowed on debtors that may be bad!

If the provision for discounts needs to be created or increased, the double-entry is:

Debit Profit and Loss Account

Credit Provision for discounts allowed account

with the amount of the increase.

If the provision for discounts allowed needs to be decreased, the double-entry is:

Debit Provision for discounts allowed account

Credit Profit and Loss Account

with the amount of the decrease.

The closing balance in the Provision for discounts allowed account is deducted from the debtors figure in the Balance Sheet. As a result, the debtors figure in the Balance Sheet will reflect the true value of debtors that will be turned into cash. Remember, the definition of current assets of a business is those assets of a business that can be converted into cash within a year.

The actual Discounts allowed account is dealt with in the normal way:

Debit Discounts allowed account

Credit Debtors account

The Discounts allowed account is a separate account from the Provision for discounts account. This is similar to the treatment of the Bad debts account and the Provision for bad debts account.

PRACTICE EXAMPLE 5

A trader commences business on 1 January 1997 and the following information has been extracted from the books:

	DEBTORS BEFORE BAD DEBTS	BAD DEBTS	PROV. FOR BAD DEBTS	PROV. FOR DISCOUNT
	€	€	€	€
y/e 31/12/97	110,000	1,700	5%	5%
y/e 31/12/98	96,000	2,000	5%	3%

Prepare the Bad debts account, Provision for bad debts account and Provision for discounts account for 1997 and 1998. Show the entries in the Profit and Loss Account and Balance Sheet for both years.

PRACTICE EXAMPLE 5 SOLUTION

BAD DEBTS ACCOUNT

Debit						**Credit**
1997	Debtors	1,700	Dec. 31 1997	Profit and Loss		1,700
1998	Debtors	2,000	Dec. 31 1998	Profit and Loss		2,000

PROVISION FOR BAD DEBTS ACCOUNT

Debit					Credit
Dec. 31 1997	Balance c/d	5,415	Dec. 31 1997	Profit and Loss	5,415
Dec. 31 1998	Profit and Loss	715	Jan. 1 1998	Balance b/d	5,415
Dec. 31 1998	Balance c/d	4,700			
		5,415			5,415
			Jan. 1 1999	Balance b/d	4,700

PROVISION FOR DISCOUNTS ALLOWED ACCOUNT

Debit					Credit
Dec. 31 1997	Balance c/d	5,144	Dec. 31 1997	Profit and Loss	5,144
Dec. 31 1998	Profit and Loss	2,465	Jan. 1 1998	Balance b/d	5,144
Dec. 31 1998	Balance c/d	2,679			
		5,144			5,144
			Jan. 1 1999	Balance b/d	2,679

PROFIT AND LOSS ACCOUNT Y/E 31 DECEMBER 1997

	Debit	Credit
	€	€
Bad debts written off	1,700	
Provision for bad debts	5,415	
Provision for discount allowed	5,144	

BALANCE SHEET Y/E 31 DECEMBER 1997

CURRENT ASSETS	€	€
Debtors	108,300	
less provision for bad debts	(5,415)	
less provision for discounts	(5,144)	97,741

PROFIT AND LOSS ACCOUNT Y/E 31 DECEMBER 1998

	Debit	Credit
	€	€
Bad debts written off	2,000	
Decrease in bad debts provision		715
Decrease in provision for discounts		2,465

BALANCE SHEET Y/E 31 DECEMBER 1998

CURRENT ASSETS	€	€
Debtors	94,000	
less provision for bad debts	(4,700)	
less provision for discounts	(2,679)	86,621

<u>Calculations</u>

<u>1997 Debtors</u>	
	110,000
less bad debts written off	(1,700)
= closing balance of debtors	108,300

Provision for bad debts is 5% of €108,300 = €5,415

Provision for discounts is 5% of (€108,300 - €5,415) = €5,144

<u>1998 Debtors</u>	
	96,000
less bad debts written off	(2,000)
= closing balance of debtors	94,000

Provision for bad debts is 5% of €94,000 = €4,700

Provision for discounts is 3% of (€94,000 - €4,700) = €2,679

NOTE: an increase in either provision is a debit in the Profit and Loss Account and a decrease is a credit in the Profit and Loss Account. Also note that the provision for discounts allowed is calculated <u>after</u> the provision for bad debts, as it is a percentage of the net debtors.

EXERCISE 1

On 1 January 1999 a trader had debtors of €40,000 and a provision for bad debts of €380. During 1999 credit sales were €86,000 and payments to debtors were €100,000 and €200 was written off as a bad debt. The trader decides at the end of the year to create a provision for bad debts of 2% of debtors. Show the relevant ledger accounts and the entries in the Profit and Loss Account and Balance Sheet for y/e 31 December 1999.

EXERCISE 2

The following information is available for y/e 31 December 1997:

Debtors at 1 January 1997	€113,000
Provision for bad debts at 1 January 1997	€4,000
Provision for discounts allowed at 1 January 1997	800
Credit sales during the year	€300,000
Payments by debtors during the year	€382,000
Bad debts written off	3,900
Discount allowed	€1,000

The trader wishes to make a provision for bad debts of 5% of closing debtors and a provision for discounts of 4%. Show the relevant ledger accounts and the entries in the Profit and Loss Account and Balance Sheet for y/e 31 December 1997.

EXERCISE 3

The following is an extract from the Trial Balance of a trader as at 31 December1999.

	Debit	Credit
	€	€
Debtors	45,000	
Bad debts written off	280	
Discount allowed	800	
Bad debts recovered		120
Provision for bad debts		1,600
Provision for discounts		2,000

The following notes appear as adjustments:

The provision for bad debts is to be adjusted to 5% of debtors and the provision for discounts is to be adjusted to 3%. Show the two Provisions accounts and the entries in the Profit and Loss Account and Balance Sheet for the relevant year end.

CHAPTER 7

Final Accounts with Adjustments

Final Accounts of a Sole Trader

So far we have learned about double-entry accounting and about some of the adjustments that need to be made to the Trial Balance. From this we should be able to draw up a Trading Account, Profit and Loss Account and Balance Sheet for a sole trader, with the necessary adjustments to the Trial Balance. Before doing so, it will be useful to recap on some important points concerning the Final Accounts of a sole trader.

The business activity of a sole trader is separate from his own private transactions. For instance, the sole trader maintains a separate bank account to record business transactions.

All money introduced by a sole trader into his business is treated as Capital. Any profit made belongs to the sole trader and is added to the Capital at the end of the accounting period.

Any withdrawals of cash or assets for the sole trader's personal use are treated as Drawings, which reduce the Capital at the end of the accounting period. Drawings are not treated as expenses in arriving at the profit or loss for the accounting period.

PRACTICE EXAMPLE 1

The following Trial Balance was extracted from the ledger of John Malone, a sole trader, as at 30 June 1999.

	Debit €	Credit €
Premises at cost	130,000	
Furniture at cost	70,000	
Accumulated depreciation: premises (1/7/98)		20,000
Accumulated depreciation: furniture (1/7/98)		14,000
Purchases and Sales	265,000	400,000
Returns	8,000	10,000
Stock at 1 July 1998	60,000	
Advertising	7,400	
Bad debts	2,000	
Bank charges	150	
Carriage in	2,000	
Discount allowed	12,000	
Discount received		15,000
Wages and salaries	56,000	
Distribution expenses	6,000	
Debtors and Creditors	39,000	34,000
Cash on hand	800	
Cash at bank	1,200	
Repairs	450	
Provision for bad debts		1,000
Long term loan		30,000
Capital as at 1 July 1998		150,000
Drawings	14,000	
	€674,000	€674,000

At the end of the year the following information is available:

1. Closing stock at 30 June 1999 is valued at €40,000.
2. Wages and salaries outstanding total €350.
3. The provision for bad debts is to be adjusted to 5% of debtors.
4. €400 of advertising relates to the following year.
5. Depreciation for y/e 30 June 1999 is to be provided as follows:
   Premises 2% p.a. of cost
   Furniture 10% p.a. reducing balance.

Prepare a Profit and Loss Account and Balance Sheet for y/e 30 June 1999.

PRACTICE EXAMPLE 1 SOLUTION

TRADING, PROFIT AND LOSS ACCOUNT OF JOHN MALONE Y/E 30 JUNE 1999

	Debit		Credit
	€	€	€
Sales	400,000		
less Sales returns	(8,000)		392,000
less Cost of sales:			
Opening stock		60,000	
Purchases	265,000		
less Purchases returns	(10,000)	255,000	
Carriage in		2,000	
		317,000	
less Closing stock		(40,000)	
Cost of sales:			(277,000)
Gross profit			115,000
Discount received			15,000
			130,000
less Expenses:			
Advertising	7,400		
less prepaid	(400)	7,000	
Bad debts		2,000	
Bank charges		150	
Discount allowed		12,000	
Wages and salaries	56,000		
add due	350	56,350	
Distribution expenses		6,000	
Repairs		450	
Increase in provision for bad debts		950	
Depreciation premises		2,600	
Depreciation furniture		5,600	(93,100)
Net profit			€36,900

NOTES:

1. Provision for bad debts:

   Provision as at 1 July 1998 €1,000
   Adjustment to 5% of debtors €1,950
   = increase in provision €950

2. Depreciation:

   Premises 2% p.a. of cost = 2% of €130,000 = €2,600
   Furniture 10% p.a. reducing balance = 10% of (€70,000 - €14,000) = €5,600

BALANCE SHEET OF JOHN MALONE Y/E 30 JUNE 1999

FIXED ASSETS	COST	ACC. DEP	NBV
	€	€	€
Premises	130,000	22,600	107,400
Furniture	70,000	19,600	50,400
			157,800
CURRENT ASSETS			
Closing stock		40,000	
Debtors	39,000		
less Provision for bad debts	(1,950)	37,050	
Cash		800	
Bank		1,200	
Advertising prepaid		400	
		79,450	
less CURRENT LIABILITIES			
Creditors	34,000		
Wages due	350	(34,350)	
Working capital			45,100
			€202,900
Financed by:			
Capital		150,000	
add Net profit		36,900	
		186,900	
less Drawings		(14,000)	172,900
Long term loan			30,000
			€202,900

Final Accounts of Companies

A company is a separate legal entity, distinct from its owners who are more commonly known as members or shareholders. Each shareholder of a company owns a number of shares in the company's Capital. The shareholders of limited companies have limited liability, meaning that they cannot be required to contribute more Capital than the value of their shares. This limited liability is one important distinction between a company and a sole trader or partnership.

Characteristics of a Limited Company

The main characteristic of a company is that of being a separate legal entity. This means that the company itself is distinct from those who own it i.e. the shareholders. This fact means that a company can sue (or be sued) in its own name and can enter into contracts in its own name. This is important for the shareholders since legal action may not easily be brought against them.

A company has perpetual life. This means that it will not cease due to changes in its membership through death, retirement or any other reason.

A company has limited liability meaning that the liability of its shareholders is limited to the amount of capital they have contributed, or agree to contribute. Private limited companies have the word 'Limited' after their name and all public limited companies have the intials 'PLC' after their name.

Formation of a Limited Company

To form a limited company in Ireland, a minimum of two persons must make an application to the Registrar of Companies situated at Dublin Castle. This application must be accompanied by certain documents, the most important of which are the **Memorandum of Association** and **Articles of Association**. The Memorandum of Association defines the company's relationship with the outside world and consists of clauses such as:

- The name of the Company, including address of registered office.
- The objects of the Company, meaning what business activities it intends to carry on.
- The share capital of the Company, including how it is divided into different classes of shares.
- The limited liability clause stating that the company possesses limited liability.

The Articles of Association set out the internal rules by which a company is governed and may deal with matters such as directors' duties, voting procedures, payment of dividends, raising of capital, etc.

Public and Private Companies

A public limited company must state in its Memorandum of Association that it is one and must end its name with the words 'Public Limited Company' or PLC. The minimum amount of shareholders for a PLC is seven and it must have a share capital of at least €30,000. Public limited companies must publish their final accounts and are under much more scrutiny from the general public than private companies. They have the right to offer and sell their shares to the public and this is the usual way that they raise capital.

Private limited companies must have at least two shareholders and end their name with the word 'Limited' or the abbreviation Ltd. Private companies cannot ask the public to subscribe for shares and they suffer restrictions on the transfer of shares to third parties. They have less onerous reporting requirements. Private companies are mostly owned and managed by small family businesses.

The management of all limited companies is in the hands of a Board of Directors who are appointed by the shareholders at the Annual General Meeting (AGM). These directors appoint a Managing Director to run the company on a day-to-day basis. The directors may get an annual fee in return for managing the company, which is treated as an expense in the Profit and Loss Account of the business.

Differences between the Accounts of Companies and Sole Traders

The Profit and Loss Account of a sole trader might look as follows:

Gross profit	€10,000
less Expenses	(€6,000)
Net profit, which is transferred to Capital account	€4,000

The Profit and Loss Account of a company might be:

Gross profit	€10,000
less Expenses	(€6,000)
Net profit	€4,000
less Dividends	(€1,500)
Retained profit	€2,500
add Retained profit at beginning of year	€600
Retained profit at end of year	€3,100

It is obvious when comparing the two Profit and Loss Accounts that the main difference arises after calculating the Net profit figure. In a sole trader's situation, the Net profit is added to his Capital in the Balance Sheet. In other words, all of the Net profit earned belongs to the sole trader and increases his Capital.

In a company's situation, some of the Net profit is used to pay dividends to the shareholders. Here the shareholders get a proportion of the profit each year. Usually not all of the profit each year is distributed in the form of dividends to shareholders. Some of the Net profit is 'retained' by the company. The advantages of retaining some profit are as follows:

1. The company can use the money to expand the business.

2. It may use it to pay off a debenture loan.

3. It may use it in future years to pay a dividend to shareholders when profit is scarce.

In the example we just looked at, €2,500 profit is retained by the company. The company would normally have retained profits from the last accounting period (in this example, €600) and this is added to this year's retained profits. The resultant figure of €3,100 represents the total retained profit of the company which is carried forward to the Balance Sheet.

The entries after the Net profit figure are arrived at in an account known as an Appropriation account. This account is an extension of the Profit and Loss Account. What is meant by the term 'appropriation of profit' is how the company allocates the profit. The first allocation may be the payment of corporation tax which is the form of taxation that a company pays. The balance left represents the amount available to shareholders for that year. Some of this is used to pay dividends and some may be transferred to a reserve. Any balance remaining will remain in the Profit and Loss Account and will be carried forward to the following year (i.e. retained profits).

The Balance Sheet of Companies

The Balance Sheet of a company is similar to that of a sole trader, except for the 'Financed by' section.

The 'Financed by' or Capital section of a sole trader's Balance Sheet might look as follows:

Capital	€50,000
Add Net profit	€2,000
	€52,000
less Drawings	(€3,000)
= Capital at end of year	€49,000

In the case of a limited company, the Capital section might look as follows;

Share capital	**Authorised**	**Issued**
50,000 ordinary shares @ €1	€70,000	€50,000
Reserves:		
Share premium		€6,000
Profit and Loss balance		€14,000
Long-term liabilities:		
10% Debentures		€80,000
		€150,000

Let us look at each of the entries in the Capital section of a company's accounts separately.

Share capital: the ownership of a company is through shares which have been issued by the company. A company may, for example, issue 10,000 shares at €1 each to an investor who wishes to purchase a stake in the company. The total amount of share capital a company can issue is governed by its Memorandum of Association. This maximum amount of share capital a company can issue is called the **authorised share capital**. This authorised figure may be increased with the agreement of shareholders. The issued share capital represents that proportion of the authorised share capital which has been taken up by the shareholders. In the Balance Sheet of a company, the authorised share capital is stated for information purposes only i.e. it is not part of the calculations to arrive at the total figure in the Balance Sheet. It is the issued share capital that forms part of the Balance Sheet calculations.

Share premium: it is common for companies to issue shares at a price in excess of their **nominal value** or **par value** which may be €1. The difference between the value at which shares are issued and the nominal value is referred to as the **share premium**. The share premium account is, in fact, a capital reserve of the company.

Reserve: this is a gain or profit that has been retained within the company. Reserves may be divided into two main categories:

1. Revenue reserves: these represent undistributed or retained *trading* profits. They can be used by the directors of the company to pay dividends in the future or for any other reason they think fit. Revenue reserves are shown under various headings, the most common being the Profit and Loss Account balance (retained profits).

2. Capital reserves: these represent profits which are not associated with the normal course of trading e.g. share premium account. These reserves cannot be distributed in the form of dividends to shareholders. They can be used to finance future expansion of the company, for example.

Profit and Loss balance: this is the figure that has been extracted from the Profit and Loss Account. It represents the retained profit of the company for this year plus any retained profit brought forward from last year. This is a revenue reserve and will appear with other reserves in the Balance Sheet at the year end.

Debentures: it is common for companies to borrow funds on a long-term basis. One important form of a long-term loan normally associated with limited companies is a debenture. The institution from which this loan is borrowed is known as a **debenture holder**. The debenture is for a fixed period of time e.g. 20 years, and a fixed rate of interest attaches to it. Debenture holders are often offered security for the amount owed in the form of a charge on the assets owned by the company. An example may be the company's freehold land. If the company defaults on interest or capital repayments, the debenture holder, under the debenture deed, would be entitled to sell the assets on which the debenture had been secured to reclaim the amount owed.

Some debentures or loans may be unsecured. This is not a common occurrence and investors may only be prepared to offer unsecured loans to very financially sound companies.

Debenture interest is usually a fixed amount and represents a business expense in the Profit and Loss Account. If a debenture loan is for a period of 20 years the company will pay a fixed interest each year and at the end of the 20 years, it will pay back the capital sum borrowed. In this case, the company may use some of its reserves to repay the capital sum. So, it should be obvious that a company needs retained profits for such purposes as this.

Another type of debenture loan is a **convertible debenture**. This means that, at the option of the company, the sum can be converted into shares at the maturity date. So instead of repaying the capital sum borrowed on maturity, the company can offer the debenture holder the equivalent value of shares in the company.

PRACTICE EXAMPLE 2

The following Trial Balance was extracted from the books of Castro PLC as at 31 December 1998.
The company has authorised share capital of 200,000 ordinary shares at €1 each.

	Debit	Credit
	€	€
Issued share capital 180,000 ordinary shares at €1 each		180,000
Profit and Loss balance at 1/1/98		46,000
Sales		821,800
Purchases	520,000	
Stock at 1/1/98	167,000	
Wages and salaries	48,000	
Directors' fees	12,000	
Rates	14,000	
Repairs	3,600	
Insurance	5,000	
Debenture interest	6,000	
Premises at cost	200,000	
Machinery at cost	176,000	
Accumulated depreciation premises 1/1/98		24,000
Accumulated depreciation machinery 1/1/98		11,400
Discounts	4,500	6,000
Debtors and Creditors	92,000	60,000
Provision for bad debts		2,000
Share premium account		20,000
General expenses	7,000	
Bank term loan		24,800
Cash on hand	2,500	
Bank		4,600
Carriage in	3,000	
10% Debenture		60,000
	€1,260,600	€1,260,600

At the end of the year, the following additional information is available:

1. Stock at 31 December 1998 is valued at €154,000.
2. An extension to the premises during the year was built by the firm's own workmen. The cost of their labour, €1,200, is included in the figure for wages and salaries. The materials, costing €4,000, were from the firm's stocks. No entry had been made in the books.
3. General expenses due and unpaid amount to €800.
4. Insurance prepaid amounts to €480.

5. Depreciation is provided as follows:

    Premises - 2% p.a. straight-line
    Machinery - 10% p.a. reducing balance

6. The bad debts provision is to be made equal to 2% of debtors.

Prepare a Trading, Profit and Loss Account and Balance Sheet for y/e 31 December 1998.

PRACTICE EXAMPLE 2 SOLUTION

TRADING, PROFIT AND LOSS ACCOUNT OF CASTRO PLC Y/E 31 DECEMBER 1998

	€	Debit €	Credit €
Sales			821,800
less Cost of Sales:			
Opening stock		167,000	
Purchases (520,000 - 4,000)		516,000	
Carriage in		3,000	
		686,000	
less Closing stock		(154,000)	
Cost of sales:			(532,000)
Gross profit			289,800
Discount received			6,000
Decrease in bad debts provision			160
			295,960
less Expenses:			
Wages and salaries	48,000		
less Labour for premises	(1,200)	46,800	
Directors' fees		12,000	
Rates		14,000	
Repairs		3,600	
Insurance	5,000		
less prepaid	(480)	4,520	
Debenture interest		6,000	
Discount allowed		4,500	
General expenses	7,000		
add due	800	7,800	
Depreciation premises		4,104	
Depreciation machinery		16,460	
			(119,784)
Net profit			176,176
Profit and Loss balance at 1/1/98			46,000
Profit and Loss balance at 31/12/98			€222,176

BALANCE SHEET OF CASTRO PLC Y/E 31 DECEMBER 1998

FIXED ASSETS	COST	ACC. DEP	NBV
	€	€	€
Premises (200,000 + 5,200)	205,200	28,104	177,096
Machinery	176,000	27,860	148,140
			325,236
CURRENT ASSETS			
Closing stock		154,000	
Debtors	92,000		
less Provision for bad debts	(1,840)	90,160	
Cash on hand		2,500	
Insurance prepaid		480	
		247,140	
less CURRENT LIABILITIES			
Creditors	60,000		
Bank term loan	24,800		
Bank overdraft	4,600		
General expenses due	800	(90,200)	
Working capital:			156,940
Total Net assets:			€482,176
Financed by:			
Share capital	Authorised	Issued	
180,000 ordinary shares at €1	200,000	180,000	
Reserves:			
Share premium account		20,000	
Profit and Loss balance at 31/12/98		222,176	422,176
Long-term liabilities:			
10% Debentures			60,000
			€482,176

NOTES:

1. In the adjustment to the Trial Balance concerning the extension to the premises, €5,200 must be added to the cost of the premises since this is capital expenditure, not revenue expenditure, and this figure is depreciated by 2% p.a. accordingly. The materials used were taken from the company's own trading stock. Therefore, these materials are not available for resale, which suggests that the Purchases figure must be reduced by €4,000. The Purchases figure in the Trading account represents the cost of purchases that are available as stock for resale.
    The wages and salaries in the Profit and Loss Account represent the wages and salaries necessary in order for the company to carry on its trading activities. €1,200 of this is not involved in carrying on trading activities, so the wages and salaries figure must be reduced.

2. After arriving at the Net profit for y/e 31 December 1998, the retained profits of last year are added to this to arrive at the total retained profits at 31 December 1998. This is a reserve in the Capital section of the Balance Sheet.

3. The debenture loan is €60,000 with a fixed rate of interest of 10% p.a. which is equal to €6,000. This amount has been paid in full during the year. If the company did not pay this amount in full, an accrual would have to be made in the accounts.

Before going on to look at another example of Final Accounts of limited companies, some more explanations are needed.

Ordinary and Preference Shares

Ordinary shares are designed for the investor who is prepared to take a relatively high level of risk in order to obtain a return on his investment. Ordinary shareholders are entitled to receive a **dividend** or **return on investment** only after other claims have been satisfied. The preference shareholders receive their dividend before the ordinary shareholders. Only if there is a remaining profit will the ordinary shareholders receive a dividend. Of course, as mentioned earlier, not all the remaining profits available to the ordinary shareholders need be distributed to them in the form of a dividend. The directors may decide to retain some of the profits which may be used by the company for expansion or for other purposes.

Ordinary shareholders will normally be given voting rights and these votes will be used to elect the board of directors at the annual general meeting of the company. In this way, the ordinary shareholders have effective control over the company's activities.

Preference shares are designed for the investor who does not wish to take a high degree of risk. This is because the preference shareholders are entitled to a fixed dividend each year. In the accounts of a company, preference shares are usually expressed as, for example, 8% Preference shares, meaning the shareholders get 8% of the value of their investment in the form of a dividend each year. Preference shareholders are not usually given voting rights within the company.

There are many different types of preference shares:

Cumulative preference shares: shareholders will get any arrears of dividends out of future profits if dividends are not paid in a particular year.

Non-cumulative preference shares: these shares do not give the right to arrears of dividend.

Redeemable preference shares: the company has the option to buy back or redeem these shares at some future date.

Intangible Assets of a Company

Intangible assets are normally defined as those assets not having a physical embodiment, unlike fixed assets that are tangible and physical. A particularly important intangible asset is **Goodwill**. This arises from factors such as good reputation or a loyal work force which enable an existing business to generate higher profits than would be expected from a similar new business. It arises in the Balance Sheet where the owner of the business paid more for the business than the mere sum of the assets. The owner of the business has put a value on the good reputation of the business in the form of goodwill.

Another intangible asset in the Balance Sheet may be a **Patent**. A patent is granted to an inventor of an item, giving him or her sole rights to make, use and sell the invention for a limited period.

Preliminary expenses may also be classified as an intangible asset. These represent the expenses that the company incurred when it was incorporated. As mentioned earlier, when a company is formed, certain documents such as the Memorandum and Articles of Association must be drawn up. Capital duty and a registration fee also have to be paid. All of this may involve the work of a specialised person and the costs of formation are known as preliminary expenses or setting up costs. However, preliminary expenses are an asset. The company has been incorporated as a result of the expense and is worth a certain amount of money upon incorporation.

All of the above intangible assets are shown in the Balance Sheet under the heading 'Intangible assets' shown after Fixed assets.

Investments

Investments are assets of a company which has invested funds in other companies or projects. They are shown as financial assets in the Balance Sheet. In return for its investment, the company will receive investment income. The investment income earned is shown in the credit column of the Profit and Loss Account. In the Trial Balance, the market value of these investments is shown in brackets. You must enter the cost of the investments in the Balance Sheet and state the market value in brackets or as a note to the accounts.

Bills Receivable and Bills Payable

Bills receivable are current assets in the Balance Sheet and represent bills of exchange receivable. A bill of exchange is an order in writing, addressed by one person to another, requiring the person to whom it is addressed to pay on demand a specified sum of money. It is similar to an 'IOU'. So, a bill receivable suggests that a person owes the company money that will be paid at a specified future date and thus it is an asset.

Bills payable are current liabilities in the Balance Sheet. The company has undertaken to pay an outsider a sum of money at a specified future date.

Valuation of Stock

Stock is valued at the lower of cost or net realisable value. **Cost** includes the purchase price plus all other costs involved to bring the stock to the company's premises. **Net realisable value** is the estimated selling price (or market value) less any further costs of sale. You must always take the lower of these two figures for the valuation of stock in the Final Accounts. This is an example of the concept of prudence.

Classification of Expenses

It is normal for companies to group expenses in the Profit and Loss Account under different headings. The headings used are usually:

*   Establishment and administration
*   Selling and distribution
*   Financial.

In the practice example that follows, expenses in the Profit and Loss Account will be classified in this way.

PRACTICE EXAMPLE 3

The following Trial Balance was extracted from the books of Domos PLC for y/e 31 December 1999:

	Debit	Credit
	€	**€**
Authorised share capital 300,000 ordinary shares at €1 each		
Issued share capital 260,000 ordinary shares at €1 each		260,000
Purchases and Sales	140,000	208,000
Returns	4,600	5,800
Premises at cost	190,000	
Fixtures and fittings at cost	50,000	
Acc. depreciation premises 1/1/99		10,800
Acc. depreciation fixtures and fittings 1/1/99		8,000
Goodwill	40,000	
Investments (market value €80,000)	76,000	
Stock 1/1/99	34,000	
Carriage in	4,800	
Rates	4,000	
Insurance	800	
Wages and salaries	24,000	
Bad debts written off	1,000	
Directors' fees	12,000	
Light and heat	1,400	
Bills payable		4,200
Audit and legal fees	760	
Motor expenses	890	
Carriage out	490	
Debtors and Creditors	16,000	13,000
Investment income		7,600
Discounts	3,000	4,200
Debenture interest	800	
Bank	22,800	
Cash on hand	860	
Stationery and printing	4,200	
Profit and Loss balance 1/1/99		28,000
Provision for bad debts		2,800
10% Debentures		60,000
Share premium		20,000
	€632,400	€632,400

The following additional information is provided:

1. Closing stock is valued at €40,000 cost. Its market value is €64,000.

2. Wages and salaries outstanding amount to €1,300.

3. Provide for debenture interest due.

4. Stock of stationery on hand is €200.

5. The bad debts provision is to be reduced by €900.

6. Rates in the Trial Balance are for the 15 month period to 31 March 2000.

7. Depreciation is to be provided as follows:

   Premises - 2% p.a. straight-line
   Fixtures and fittings - 10% p.a. reducing balance.

8. Provide for directors' fees due of €400.

Prepare a Trading, Profit and Loss Account and Balance Sheet for y/e 31 December 1999.

PRACTICE EXAMPLE 3 SOLUTION

TRADING, PROFIT AND LOSS ACCOUNT OF DOMOS PLC Y/E 31 DECEMBER 1999

	€	Debit €	Credit €
Sales	208,000		
less Sales returns	(4,600)		203,400
less Cost of sales:			
Opening stock		34,000	
Purchases	140,000		
less Purchases returns	(5,800)	134,200	
Carriage in		4,800	
		173,000	
less Closing stock		(40,000)	
Cost of sales:			(133,000)
Gross profit			70,400
Discount received			4,200
Investment income			7,600
Decrease in bad debts provision			900
less Expenses:			83,100
Establishment and administration:			
Rates	4,000		
less prepaid	(800)	3,200	
Insurance		800	
Wages and salaries	24,000		
add due	1,300	25,300	
Directors' fees	12,000		
add due	400	12,400	
Light and heat		1,400	
Stationery and printing	4,200		
less prepaid	(200)	4,000	
Depreciation premises		3,800	
Depreciation fixtures and fittings		4,200	(55,100)
Selling and distribution:			
Motor expenses		890	
Carriage out		490	
Discounts allowed		3,000	(4,380)
Financial:			
Bad debts written off		1,000	
Audit and legal fees		760	
Debenture interest	800		
add due	5,200	6,000	(7,760)
Net profit			15,860
Profit and Loss balance 1/1/99			28,000
Profit and Loss balance 31/12/99			€43,860

BALANCE SHEET OF DOMOS PLC Y/E 31 DECEMBER 1999

FIXED ASSETS	COST	ACC. DEP	NBV
	€	€	€
Premises	190,000	14,600	175,400
Fixtures and fittings	50,000	12,200	37,800
			213,200
INTANGIBLE ASSETS			
Goodwill			40,000
FINANCIAL ASSETS			
Investments (market value €80,000)			76,000
CURRENT ASSETS			
Closing stock		40,000	
Debtors	16,000		
less Bad debts provision	(1,900)	14,100	
Bank		22,800	
Cash on hand		860	
Rates prepaid		800	
Stock of stationery on hand		200	
		78,760	
less CURRENT LIABILITIES			
Creditors	13,000		
Bills payable	4,200		
Wages and salaries due	1,300		
Directors' fees due	400		
Debenture interest due	5,200	(24,100)	
Working capital:			54,660
Total Net assets			€383,860
Financed by:			
Share capital:	Authorised	Issued	
260,000 ordinary shares at €1 each	300,000	260,000	
Reserves			
Share premium account		20,000	
Profit and Loss balance 31/12/99		43,860	323,860
Long-term liabilities:			
10% Debentures			60,000
			€383,860

EXERCISE 1

The following Trial Balance was extracted from the books of John Noone, a sole trader, as at 30 June 1999:

	Debit	Credit
	€	€
Purchases and Sales	40,000	68,000
Stock 1/7/98	12,000	
Returns	400	860
Discounts	480	690
Carriage in	200	
Rent and rates	3,500	
Wages and salaries	12,000	
Motor expenses	390	
Premises at cost	70,000	
Acc. depreciation premises 1/7/98		20,000
Motor vehicles at cost	23,000	
Acc. depreciation motor vehicles 1/7/98		3,200
Bad debts written off	800	
Provision for bad debts		1,200
Drawings	400	
Debtors and Creditors	13,000	9,200
Advertising	250	
Bank	12,500	
Cash on hand	400	
Repairs	830	
Capital		87,000
	€190,150	€190,150

The following additional information is available:

1. Stock at 30 June 1999 is valued at €15,000.
2. The rent and rates figure is for the 15 month period to 30 September 1999.
3. The owner, John Noone, made drawings of stock during the year of €800. No entry had been made in the books.
4. Depreciation is to be provided as follows:
    Premises - 2% p.a. straight-line,
    Motor vehicles - 20% p.a. reducing balance.
5. The provision for bad debts is to be adjusted to 5% of debtors.

Prepare a Trading, Profit and Loss Account and Balance Sheet for y/e 30 June 1999.

EXERCISE 2

The following Trial Balance was extracted from the books of Boyle PLC as at 31 December 1999:

	Debit €	Credit €
Authorised share capital, 100,000 ordinary shares at €1 each		
Issued share capital 80,000 ordinary shares at €1 each		80,000
Premises (cost €80,000)	65,000	
Plant and machinery (cost €40,000)	32,000	
Goodwill	25,000	
Profit and Loss balance 1/1/99		26,300
Investments (market value €70,000)	58,000	
Carriage out	1,500	
Purchases and Sales	140,000	208,000
Bank		13,000
Bills receivable	1,400	
Debtors and Creditors	16,000	11,000
Stock 1/1/99	12,400	
Salaries and wages	18,000	
Light and heat	8,000	
Rent and rates	2,000	
Audit and legal fees	700	
Advertising	1,200	
Motor expenses	900	
Provision for bad debts		1,200
Discounts allowed	800	
Cash on hand	400	
Debenture interest	3,200	
Bank charges	500	
Directors' fees	10,000	
Investment income		2,500
10% Debentures		40,000
Share premium		15,000
	€397,000	€397,000

The following additional information is provided:

1. Stock at 31 December 1999 is valued at €14,000.
2. Goods costing €2,000 were purchased on credit. These have been included in stocks but no entry has been made in the books.
3. Provide for rent due of €600.
4. Advertising prepaid is €300.
5. The debtors figure includes an amount of €800 that is written off as a bad debt. No entry for this has been made in the books. The bad debts provision is to be adjusted to 10% of debtors.

6.   Provide for debenture interest outstanding.

7.   Depreciation is to be provided as follows:

Premises - 4% p.a. of cost,
Plant and machinery - 20% p.a. reducing balance.

Prepare a Trading, Profit and Loss Account and Balance Sheet for y/e 31 December 1999.

EXERCISE 3

The following is a Trial Balance from the books of Salt PLC as at 31 December 1999. The authorised share capital of the company is 300,000 ordinary shares at €1 each.

	Debit	Credit
	€	€
Issued share capital 270,000 ordinary shares at €1 each		270,000
Freehold land	170,000	
Motor vehicles at cost	36,000	
Acc. depreciation motor vehicles 1/1/99		7,200
Goodwill	10,000	
Patents	5,000	
Purchases and Sales	86,000	132,520
Stock 1/1/99	15,000	
Share premium		30,000
Rent and rates	4,400	
Insurance	800	
Motor expenses	560	
Debtors and Creditors	14,000	11,000
Light and heat	3,200	
Wages and salaries	15,000	
Profit and Loss balance 1/1/99	4,000	
Bills payable		8,000
Directors' fees	8,000	
Bad debts recovered		900
Discounts	2,300	1,900
Audit and legal fees	480	
Carriage out	960	
Debenture interest	3,000	
Bank charges	420	
Investments (market value €90,000)	86,000	
Investment income		2,000
Provision for bad debts		2,000
Bank	40,000	
Cash on hand	400	
10% Debentures		40,000
	€505,520	€505,520

The following additional information is available:

1. Closing stock at 31 December 1999 is valued at cost, €20,000, with a market value of €18,000.
2. The provision for bad debts is to be adjusted to 5% of Debtors.
3. Rent and rates outstanding is €600.
4. Motor expenses include €200 paid for the collection of goods purchased by the Company.
5. Provide for debenture interest due.
6. Insurance prepaid is €160.
7. Depreciation is to be provided on the motor vehicles at 20% p.a. reducing balance.

Prepare a Trading, Profit and Loss Account and Balance Sheet of Salt PLC for y/e
31 December 1999.

EXERCISE 4

The following is a Trial Balance extracted from the books of ABC PLC for y/e 30 June 1999.
The authorised share capital of the Company is 300,000 ordinary shares at €1 each and 100,000
8% preference shares at €1 each.

	Debit €	Credit €
Issued share capital:		
200,000 ordinary shares at €1 each		200,000
80,000 preference shares at €1 each		80,000
Freehold land	130,000	
Premises (cost €100,000)	80,000	
Motor vehicles (cost €42,000)	36,000	
Preliminary expenses	2,500	
Purchases and Sales	76,000	92,000
Rent and rates	480	
Motor expenses	500	
Insurance	1,200	
Bank charges	200	
Debtors and Creditors	10,000	12,400
Provision for bad debts		250
Discounts	400	360
Rent received		800
Directors' fees	13,000	
Goodwill	26,000	
Profit and Loss balance 1/7/98	10,000	
Stock 1/7/98	4,670	
Debenture interest	2,500	
Share premium account		5,000
15% Debentures		20,000
Bank	14,000	
Cash on hand	860	
Advertising	490	
Bad debts written off	410	
Bills receivable	2,500	
Bank term loan		30,000
Import duties	600	
Stationery	230	
Wages and salaries	28,000	
Carriage out	270	
	€440,810	€440,810

The following additional information is available:

1. Stock at 30 June 1999 is valued at €7,000.

2. Provide for advertising prepaid of €100.

3. The provision for bad debts is to be increased by €150.

4. Provide for debenture interest due.

5. A Christmas bonus of stock has been given to employees costing €1,600. The closing stock figure is adjusted, but no other entry has been made in the accounts.

6. Provide for rent received outstanding of €50.

7. Depreciation is provided as follows:

   Premises - 4% p.a. of cost,
   Motor vehicles - 20% p.a. book value.

8. An extension to the Premises was built during the year by the firm's own workmen. The cost of their labour, €2,600, is included in the figure for wages and salaries. The materials, costing €4,000, were from the firm's stocks. No entry has been made in the books.

Prepare a Trading, Profit and Loss Account and Balance Sheet of ABC PLC for y/e 30 June 1999.

EXERCISE 5

The following is a Trial Balance of Mayberry PLC for y/e 31 December 1999. The authorised share capital of the Company is 300,000 ordinary shares at €1 each.

	Debit €	Credit €
Issued share capital: 180,000 ordinary shares at €1 each		180,000
Buildings (cost €90,000)	86,000	
Motor vehicles (cost €40,000)	25,000	
Goodwill	7,000	
Debtors and Creditors	10,000	9,000
Purchases and Sales	84,000	109,100
Returns	4,000	4,800
Profit and Loss balance 1/1/99		48,000
Stock 1/1/99	56,000	
Bad debts	2,800	
Provision for bad debts		200
Debenture interest	680	
Wages and salaries	38,000	
Investments (market value €12,000)	15,800	
Rent received		3,200
Selling expenses	2,600	
General administration expenses	4,300	
Investment income		4,200
Preliminary expenses	800	
Patents and trade marks	2,000	
Bank	28,000	
Cash on hand	890	
Advertising	400	
Discounts	400	800
Carriage in	800	
Carriage out	250	
Share premium account		10,000
5% Debentures		20,000
Directors' fees	14,500	
Bank charges	280	
Hire of office equipment	3,000	
Commissions	1,800	
	€389,300	€389,300

The following additional information is available:

1. Stock at 31 December 1999 is valued at cost, €40,000, with a market value of €52,000.

2. Provide for directors' fees due of €860.

3. The amount in respect of the hire of office equipment covers the period ending 30 June 2000.

4. Included in the debtors figure is an extra bad debt of €800 which is to be written off. The provision for bad debts is to be adjusted to 5% of closing debtors.

5. Provide for rent received prepaid of €200.

6. Wages and salaries due amount to €490.

7. Provide for debenture interest due.

8. The figure for carriage in includes the cost of delivery of a motor vehicle during the year of €50. This extra cost is not to be depreciated.

9. Depreciation is to be provided as follows:

   Buildings - 2% p.a. straight-line,
   Motor vehicles - 20% p.a. reducing balance.

Prepare a Trading, Profit and Loss Account and Balance Sheet of Mayberry PLC for y/e 31 December 1999.

CHAPTER 8

Interpretation of Final Accounts

We have already described the role of accounting in providing financial information to help people make decisions. So far we have been concerned with the collection and analysis of accounting information rather than its interpretation and use. The preparation of financial statements is not an end in itself. It is important to be able to analyse and interpret the financial results. The people who will be interested in the interpretation of financial statements include bankers, investors, directors, employees, creditors and the Government. Their particular interests will vary and it is important that each user is able to draw his own conclusions from the financial statements.

The main technique used in interpreting financial information is ratio analysis. The main emphasis in this chapter will be on using accounting ratios as a means of drawing logical conclusions from accounting statements, thus enabling more informed decisions to be made by the users of accounts.

A **ratio** is a relationship in quantity, number or degree between one thing and another. It is a measure, often expressed in percentage terms. Ratios, once calculated, should be subject to comparison. For example, to state that a company's net profit percentage is 20% is meaningless in itself. We would need the company's net profit percentage for past years, or the net profit percentage of similar firms, in order to be able to draw adequate and useful conclusions. Therefore, once ratios are calculated, they need to be compared to the company's own past performance, or to those of similar firms, or to the industry's average results.

There are many problems in comparing ratios from one period to another. Just because a ratio is currently better than it has been in the past, that does not necessarily mean that it is acceptable now. The past result may have been totally unsatisfactory. Another problem with comparison with past periods is that the economic environment may have changed dramatically thus giving misleading results.

To counteract these drawbacks, some businesses compare their financial ratios with planned performance. This means that a business's future plans are expressed in terms of ratios. The actual resulting ratios are compared with the forecast ratios.

One of the most useful methods of comparison is for a business to compare its ratio with that of another business in the same industry. But, of course, this may also have its problems. For example, another business may draw up its accounts in a slightly different manner making it difficult to compare like with like.

Despite all these problems, ratios are a good guide to a company's performance, but do remember that they are only a guide. In essence, they provide support for other information.

Classification of Ratios

Ratios are usually classified according to the particular aspect of the business they seek to address. In this chapter, ratios will be considered under these headings:

- Profitability
- Liquidity
- Activity.

The following example will be used to illustrate the ratios:

TRADING, PROFIT AND LOSS ACCOUNT OF JONES PLC Y/E 31 DECEMBER 1999

	Debit	Credit
	€	€
Sales		75,000
less Cost of sales:		
Opening stock	5,600	
Purchases	42,400	
	48,000	
less Closing stock	(4,000)	
Cost of sales:		(44,000)
Gross profit		31,000
less expenses		(20,400)
Net profit		€10,600

BALANCE SHEET OF JONES PLC Y/E 31 DECEMBER 1999

FIXED ASSETS	€	€	€
(at cost less depreciation)			
Premises			140,000
Machinery			80,000
			220,000
CURRENT ASSETS			
Closing stock		4,000	
Debtors		12,000	
Bank and cash		4,800	
		20,800	
less CURRENT LIABILITIES			
Creditors	2,800		
Accruals	400	(3,200)	
Working capital:			17,600
Total Net assets:			€237,600
Financed by:			
Issued share capital:			
140,000 ordinary shares at €1 each			140,000
Reserves:			
Profit and Loss balance			10,600
Share premium			27,000
Long-term liabilities:		€	
10% Debenture			60,000
			€237,600

Profitability Ratios

These ratios relate the profit of the business to other figures in an attempt to assess the effectiveness of the business in achieving its main objective, which is to generate a profit.

Gross profit percentage: this expresses gross profit as a percentage of sales. It is also called the **gross margin**.

The formula is:

$$\text{Gross profit \%} = \frac{\text{Gross Profit}}{\text{Sales}} \times 100$$

For Jones PLC it would give:

$$\text{Gross profit \%} = \frac{€31,000}{€75,000} \times 100 = 41.3\%$$

It indicates the efficiency of the purchasing or producing department as well as the pricing policy of the business. A low gross profit percentage would be a sign of inefficiency of operation and/or poor pricing policy. It is difficult to comment on a result of 41.3% in isolation. It would need to be compared with previous results, projected future results and other businesses in the same industry. The type of activity the company is carrying on would also need to be known. For instance, if the company were a food supermarket, we would expect a low gross profit percentage. However, if it were in the jewellery trade, a high gross profit percentage would be expected.

If there were a number of different classes of products sold, we would need to obtain the gross profit percentage for each class of product.

This ratio should not be confused with mark up.

Mark up expresses gross profit as a percentage of cost of sales.

In Jones PLC, the mark up is calculated as:

$$\text{Mark up} = \frac{\text{Gross Profit}}{\text{Cost of Sales}} \times 100$$

Net profit percentage: this expresses the net profit as a percentage of sales.

$$\text{Net profit \%} = \frac{\text{Net Profit}}{\text{Sales}} \times 100$$

For Jones PLC it would give:

$$\text{Net profit \%} = \frac{€10,600}{€75,000} \times 100 = 14.1\%$$

The ratio indicates the efficiency of the business after deducting all expenses. If taxation is involved, the net profit is usually taken before tax. Of course, a result of 14.1% cannot be commented on without further information about the company. If there is a large gap between the gross profit % and the net profit %, it suggests that expenses are high in relation to all other figures. A more detailed analysis of the expenses may be needed in this case and it may be necessary to express each category of expense as a percentage of the sales figure.

Return on capital employed: this is perhaps the most important ratio of all in assessing the company's efficiency in generating profits. It relates the net profit to the level of investment used to earn it, i.e. the Capital of the company. There are several variations of this ratio; some take net profit before tax and others take profit after tax. Some take capital employed as including long-term liabilities while others exclude long-term liabilities. The definition depends on the use to which the ratio is to be put. The important matter is consistency from year to year and from business to business.

For simplicity, we will take the net profit and express it as a percentage of the total capital employed:

$$\text{Return on capital employed} = \frac{\text{Net profit}}{\text{Total Capital Employed}} \times 100$$

For Jones PLC, the result is:

$$\text{Return on capital employed} = \frac{€10,600}{€237,600} \times 100 = 4.46\%$$

The higher the ratio, the better. It shows the efficiency of the company to generate profit from the capital available for this. The figure of 4.46% seems quite low here. It suggests for every €100 capital, the company earns €4.46 profit. This may not be satisfactory compared with investing the money in a bank deposit account which could earn a higher return with less risk. The return on capital employed should be much higher than the return on a bank deposit account as there is a greater degree of risk involved. The higher the level of risk, the higher the expected returns should be. The return on capital employed ratio may also be called the **return on investment ratio**.

Liquidity Ratios

These ratios assess the ability of the business to meet its short-term financial obligations.

Current ratio or **Working capital ratio:** this ratio shows the relationship between current assets and current liabilities. It is calculated as:

Working capital ratio = $\dfrac{\text{Current Assets}}{\text{Current Liabilities}}$

or   Current assets : Current liabilities.

For Jones PLC, the result is:

Working capital ratio =   €20,800 : €3,200

= 6.5 : 1

The ratio indicates the extent to which the current assets will cover the current liabilities in the short-term. The above result, at a glance, indicates that Jones PLC is in a good liquidity position in the short-term. Its current assets, if converted into cash, will be able to pay its current liabilities 6.5 times over.

A working capital ratio in the region of 2:1 is generally considered acceptable. This suggests that a business has twice as many current assets as current liabilities and so should be able to pay its current liabilities if the need arose. On the other hand, too high a Working capital ratio, as for Jones PLC, may be an indication of poor management with too many resources tied up in current assets. In Jones PLC, it can be seen that the reason for such a high current asset figure is mainly due to the debtors figure of €12,000. This is high when compared to the creditors figure and suggests that the company does not have a strict credit control policy.

Before we can make a definite comment on the above result, we would need more information about the company, i.e. the type of business it is in. For example, a supermarket may have a low Working capital ratio because it turns stock over quickly and has few credit customers. A manufacturer may have a high Working capital ratio because it tends to hold quite large stocks and mostly sells on credit.

Liquidity ratio: this is also called the **Acid test ratio** or **Quick ratio**. This tests the ability of the business to meet its current liabilities without having to sell its stock to do so. Stock is excluded from current assets as it is generally the most difficult of all current assets to convert into cash quickly. The ratio is calculated as:

Liquidity ratio = Current assets less stock : Current liabilities

For Jones PLC, the result is:

Liquidity ratio = (€20,800 - €4,000) : €3,200

= 5.25 : 1

This is a high ratio for the company. It means that it can cover its current liabilities 5.25 times without selling its stock. The generally accepted liquidity ratio is 1 : 1, meaning that current assets less stock should equal current liabilities. As with the Working capital ratio, too high a liquidity ratio implies poor management and under utilisation of working capital. Again, we would need more information about the company to make an adequate comment, as considerable differences are found among various types of businesses.

Both the Working capital ratio and the Liquidity ratio are always expressed as x:1. The use of this allows for easy comparison from year to year and from business to business.

Activity Ratios

These try to assess the effectiveness of the business in using its assets to the full.

Stock turnover: this ratio indicates how many times a business turns over its stock in a given period of time. The ratio is calculated as:

$$\text{Stock turnover} = \frac{\text{Cost of Sales}}{\text{Average Stock}}$$

For Jones PLC, the result is:

$$\text{Stock turnover} = \frac{€44,000}{(€5,600 + €4,000)/2}$$

$$= \frac{€44,000}{€4,800}$$

$$= 9.16 \text{ times}$$

The average stock is calculated by adding the opening and closing stocks and dividing by 2. The result above means that the company turns over its stock 9.16 times in the year. Another angle to this is to say that the stock is replaced about every 39 days, or the company has its stock for 39 days before it is sold. It is difficult to comment on this without knowing the nature of the business of the company. For example, in a supermarket the Stock turnover ratio would be high, indicating that stock remains on the premises for a short period before it is sold. In the jewellery trade, the Stock turnover would be low, suggesting that stock is only bought in a few times during the year and so stock can remain on the premises for a long time before it is sold.

A variation of this ratio is called the **Stock holding period**. It identifies the average length of time stock is held before it is sold. The formula is:

$$\text{Stock holding period} = \frac{\text{Average Stock}}{\text{Cost of Sales}} \times 365 \text{ (in days)}$$

For Jones PLC, the result is:

$$\text{Stock holding period} = \frac{€4,800}{€44,000} \times 365 \text{ (in days)}$$

$$= 39.8 \text{ days}$$

It gives the same information as the Stock turnover ratio. It means that the company replaces its stock 9.16 times a year or every 39.8 days.

A high Stock turnover ratio is not necessarily better than a low ratio or vice versa. It depends on the business activity of the company. A high Stock turnover ratio indicates that the business keeps small amounts of stock in comparison with sales and buys in more often. A low Stock turnover suggests that the business keeps large amounts of stock in comparison with sales and buys in less often during the year.

Stock holding is expensive in terms of storage costs, money tied up and the danger of obsolescence. Having too little stock may mean that the business will miss out on trade discounts for bulk buying or lose custom through inadequate stocking levels. Therefore it is important that each business keeps its stock at an optimum, practical level, bearing in mind customer needs and the costs involved in storage.

Debtors collection period or **Debtors ratio:** this ratio expresses the average length of credit given to customers, or the average length of time it takes to convert debtors into cash. The formula is:

$$\text{Debtors collection period} = \frac{\text{Debtors}}{\text{Credit sales}} \times 365 \text{ (in days)}$$

For Jones PLC, the result is:

$$\text{Debtors collection period} = \frac{€12,000}{€75,000} \times 365 \text{ (in days)}$$

$$= 58.4 \text{ days}$$

It is assumed in the above that the sales figure of €75,000 consists of credit sales with no cash sales. The figure of 58.4 days may seem to be a long period for debtors to pay. Again, to comment adequately, we would need to know the type of business activity being carried on. It may be the case that Jones PLC must offer this length of credit in order to attract custom, but too high a credit period may mean a poor credit control policy. Giving credit is expensive in terms of money being tied up in debtors and carries the increased risk of bad debts. Selling on credit may be necessary in some businesses in order to get custom. As with stock levels, each business must achieve a balance between the costs of giving credit and the rewards associated with increased custom.

Creditors payment period or **Creditors ratio:** this ratio expresses the average length of credit taken by the business in paying its creditors. The formula is:

$$\text{Creditors payment period} = \frac{\text{Creditors}}{\text{Credit purchases}} \times 365 \text{ (in days)}$$

For Jones PLC, the result is:

$$\text{Creditors payment period} = \frac{€2,800}{€42,400} \times 365 \text{ (in days)}$$

$$= 24.1 \text{ days}$$

It is assumed that all purchases are credit purchases. Again, it is difficult to comment on this ratio in isolation. However, it can be seen that Jones PLC pays its creditors much more quickly than it receives payment from its debtors. A high payment period may be good or bad for the company. A high payment period may suggest that the company is receiving maximum benefit from free credit and using its creditors as a source of finance instead of a bank loan. However, there is a danger associated with a high payment period. It may result in suppliers refusing to give cash discounts for prompt payment or in some suppliers refusing to supply goods on credit to the company. Again, each business must strike a practical balance between the costs of losing discounts and the rewards associated with cheap credit.

PRACTICE EXAMPLE 1

The Final Accounts of Parke Ltd, a small food retailer, for the last two years are as follows:

TRADING, PROFIT AND LOSS ACCOUNT FOR Y/E 31 DECEMBER

	1998	1999
	€	€
Sales	10,900	12,400
less Cost of sales	(6,300)	(6,900)
Gross profit	4,600	5,500
less Expenses	(3,100)	(4,300)
Net profit	€1,500	€1,200

BALANCE SHEET Y/E 31 DECEMBER

	1998		1999	
	€	€	€	€
FIXED ASSETS				
(cost less depreciation)				
Land and buildings	25,000		26,000	
Plant and equipment	2,100	27,100	2,900	28,900
CURRENT ASSETS				
Stock	2,600		1,800	
Debtors	2,300		1,900	
Cash	100		190	
	5,000		3,890	
less CURRENT LIABILITIES				
Creditors	(1,000)		(1,400)	
Accruals	(200)		(320)	
Bank overdraft	(3,000)		(1,800)	
Working Capital:		800		370
Total Net assets:		€27,900		€29,270
Financed by:				
Share capital		24,000		26,500
Reserves:				
Profit and Loss balance		1,500		1,200
Long-term liabilities:				
Long-term loan		2,400		1,570
		€27,900		€29,270

The opening stock as at 1 January 1998 is valued at €2,000.

Calculate each of the following for 1998 and 1999:

1. Gross profit %
2. Net profit %
3. Return on capital employed
4. Working capital ratio
5. Liquidity ratio
6. Stock turnover.

Comment on the state of affairs of the above company.

PRACTICE EXAMPLE 1 SOLUTION

1. Gross profit % = $\dfrac{\text{Gross Profit}}{\text{Sales}} \times 100$

    $1998 \quad = \dfrac{\text{€4,600}}{\text{€10,900}} \times 100 = 42.2\%$

    $1999 \quad = \dfrac{\text{€5,500}}{\text{€12,400}} \times 100 = 44.3\%$

The ratio has increased slightly in 1999 for Parke Ltd. This implies that on a comparison of sales with cost of sales, the company is doing better in 1999 as compared to 1998. There has been an increase in sales without the same percentage increase in cost of sales. It could mean that the company has increased its selling price in 1999, or that it has a better pricing policy. Also, it could mean that it is getting its goods cheaper in 1999. For the type of business the company is in, a Gross profit percentage of over 40% seems quite satisfactory. However, a close watch would need to be kept on expenses which are not taken into account here.

2. Net profit % = $\dfrac{\text{Net Profit}}{\text{Sales}} \times 100$

    $1998 \quad = \dfrac{\text{€1,500}}{\text{€10,900}} \times 100 = 13.7\%$

    $1999 \quad = \dfrac{\text{€1,200}}{\text{€12,400}} \times 100 = 9.6\%$

The ratio has fallen dramatically in 1999. This means that the company is less profitable in 1999, as compared to 1998, despite the Gross profit % increasing. This, of course, is due to much higher expenses in 1999. Even though sales increased in 1999, total expenses increased by a greater percentage. Investigation into expenses needs to be carried out to see which expenses in particular are the cause of the overall increase. It is not to the benefit of the company to generate more sales if this results in a greater increase in expenses. The expenses seem to be in excess of what the company can afford.

For a food retailing business, a Net profit percentage of over 9% may seem satisfactory, given the low mark up that exists on food. But the company would need to investigate this further to prevent any more decreases in the Net profit percentage.

3. Return on capital employed = $\dfrac{\text{Net Profit}}{\text{Total capital employed}} \times 100$

$$1998 = \frac{\text{€}1,500}{\text{€}27,900} \times 100 = 5.37\%$$

$$1999 = \frac{\text{€}1,200}{\text{€}29,270} \times 100 = 4.09\%$$

The ratio has worsened in 1999 due to the fall in profitability. A result of 4% or 5% is quite unsatisfactory. The company would be better off investing its Capital in a bank deposit account where there is no risk attached.

In present times, a business should have a Return on capital employed of at least 10% to make it worthwhile trading. The higher the risk in trading, the higher the Return on capital employed should be. A profit of €1,200 in 1999 is not adequate, taking into account that the company has an investment of €29,270 to earn this. The company needs to find ways to increase its net profit figure by either reducing expenses, increasing its selling price, attracting new customers or a combination of all these.

4. Working capital ratio = Current assets : Current liabilities

    1998 = €5,000 : €4,200 = 1.19 : 1

    1999 = €3,890 : €3,520 = 1.10 : 1

This also suggests a worsening situation in 1999. Generally, an acceptable ratio is 2 : 1. However, retailers tend to be lower as they turn their stock over fairly quickly and have few debtors. But in this company the debtors figure is substantial for both years relative to sales generated, and the stock figure is relatively high. This is unusual for a retailer where most of sales should be for cash. Given the result above, the company would not be able to pay its short-term liabilities without selling most of its current assets. The reason for the relatively high level of current liabilities is the bank overdraft which is used as a source of finance. To improve the position, the company should try to receive payment from its debtors more quickly and use this money to pay off the bank overdraft. If this is not possible, it should convert its bank overdraft into shares or a long-term loan. This would, of course, only improve its short-term liquidity, not its long-term liquidity.

5. Liquidity ratio = Current assets less stock : Current liabilities

    1998 = €2,400 : €4,200 = 0.57 : 1

    1999 = €2,090 : €3,520 = 0.59 : 1

Even with a slight improvement in 1999, the liquidity ratio seems inadequate for both years. The company is unable to meet its current liabilities without selling its stock. This is a more stringent test of liquidity than the Working capital ratio. The reason for excluding stock is that, in most types of businesses, stock is not very liquid, i.e. it is difficult to turn into cash quickly.

6. Stock turnover $= \dfrac{\text{Cost of Sales}}{\text{Average Stock}}$

$$1998 = \frac{\text{€}6,300}{(\text{€}2,000 + \text{€}2,600)/2} = 2.7 \text{ times}$$

$$1999 = \frac{\text{€}6,900}{(\text{€}2,600 + \text{€}1,800)/2} = 3.1 \text{ times}$$

This is extremely low for a food retailer. On average, the company only replaces its stock about 3 times a year, or every 4 months. It suggests that the stock figure is too high relative to the value of sales generated. The stock is on the premises for about 4 months before it is sold. This is a small retailing business and the reason for such high stock levels may be the need to offer customers sufficient choice and/or to make use of trade discounts for bulk buying. Stock holding is expensive and the company should try to lower its stock levels to reduce costs and the danger of stock becoming damaged and out of date. The company should use the money tied up in stock to reduce the bank overdraft so as to not worsen its liquidity position.

PRACTICE EXAMPLE 2

James Doyle started a business on 1 January 1999 with €60,000 Capital. The following information was supplied by him on 31 December 1999:

Period of credit given to debtors	40 days
Working capital ratio	2:1
Liquidity ratio	1:1
Drawings during the year	€10,000
Mark up	20%
Working capital	€30,000
Stock turnover (based on closing stock)	7 times
Depreciation machinery	€4,000
Total expenses (excluding depreciation)	€6,500

Machinery is the only fixed asset and is depreciated at 10% p.a. straight-line for the full year.

Current assets consist of stock, debtors and bank.

Creditors is the only current liability.

Prepare a Trading, Profit and Loss Account and Balance Sheet for Mr Doyle for y/e 31 December 1999 in as much detail as possible.

PRACTICE EXAMPLE 2 SOLUTION

Before preparing the accounts of Mr Doyle, we must work out some figures based on the information given. It will then be possible to prepare the account in 'skeleton' form and fill in the missing figures.

Working capital = €30,000, i.e. current assets less current liabilities.

Working capital ratio = 2:1

This implies that the total current assets are €60,000 and the current liabilities are €30,000.

Liquidity ratio = 1:1 i.e. current assets less stock = current liabilities.

This implies that stock = €30,000

$$\text{Stock turnover (based on closing stock)} = \frac{\text{Cost of Sales}}{\text{Cl. stock}} = 7 \text{ times}$$

$$= \frac{\text{Cost of Sales}}{€30,000} = 7 \text{ times}$$

This implies that Cost of sales = €210,000

Mark up = 20% i.e. Gross profit is 20% of Cost of sales.

Gross profit = 20% of €210,000

= €42,000

Sales = Cost of sales + Gross profit

= €252,000

Period of credit given to debtors $= \dfrac{\text{Debtors}}{\text{Cr. Sales}} \times 365$

We can assume that all sales are on credit.

$$= \dfrac{\text{Debtors}}{\text{€}252{,}000} \times 365 = 40 \text{ days}$$

This implies that debtors = €27,616

Machinery is the only fixed asset, whose depreciation is €4,000 which equals 10% of cost. Therefore the cost of machinery for the Balance Sheet is €40,000.

We are now in a position to do the accounts of Mr Doyle.

TRADING, PROFIT AND LOSS ACCOUNT OF MR DOYLE Y/E 31 DECEMBER 1999

	Debit	Credit
	€	€
Sales		252,000
less Cost of sales		(210,000)
Gross Profit		42,000
less Expenses*	22,000*	
less Depreciation machinery	4,000	(26,000)
Net profit*		€16,000*

BALANCE SHEET OF MR DOYLE Y/E 31 DECEMBER 1999

FIXED ASSETS	COST	ACC. DEP	NBV
	€	€	€
Machinery	40,000	4,000	36,000
CURRENT ASSETS			
Stock		30,000	
Debtors		27,616	
Bank (balancing figure)		2,384	
		60,000	
less CURRENT LIABILITIES			
Creditors		(30,000)	
Working capital:			30,000
Total Net assets			€66,000
Financed by:			
Capital		60,000	
Add Net profit*		16,000	
		76,000	
less Drawings (known)		(10,000)	
			€66,000

* The total net assets of the Balance Sheet equal €66,000.

Capital + Net profit - Drawings =	€66,000
€60,000 + Net profit - €10,000 =	€66,000

This implies that net profit = €16,000.

When this Net profit is inserted in the Profit and Loss Account, expenses (excluding depreciation) equal €22,000.

EXERCISE 1

The following figures were taken from the final accounts of Murphy Ltd on 31 December 1999:

Stock 1 Jan. 1999	€42,000
Purchases	€360,000
Sales	€440,000
Stock 31 Dec. 1999	€38,000
Current assets	€56,000
Current liabilities	€36,000
Expenses	€32,000
Total Capital employed	€500,000

You are required to calculate the following ratios:

1. Stock turnover
2. Gross profit %
3. Net profit %
4. Working capital ratio

5. Liquidity ratio

6. Return on capital employed.

EXERCISE 2

Franco Ltd, a major retail company, has produced the following accounts for y/e 31 December 1998 and 31 December 1999:

TRADING, PROFIT AND LOSS ACCOUNT Y/E 31 DECEMBER

	1998	1999
	€	€
Sales	510,000	1,325,000
less Cost of sales	(320,000)	(900,000)
Gross profit	190,000	425,000
less Expenses	(152,000)	(215,000)
Net profit	€38,000	€210,000

BALANCE SHEET Y/E 31 DECEMBER

	1998		1999	
	€	€	€	€
FIXED ASSETS				
(cost less depreciation)				
Land and buildings		178,000		205,000
Fixtures and fittings		50,000		70,000
		228,000		275,000
CURRENT ASSETS				
Stock	97,000		127,000	
Debtors	8,000		16,000	
Bank	9,000		54,000	
Prepayments	4,000		6,000	
	118,000		203,000	
less CURRENT LIABILITIES				
Creditors	(72,000)		(80,000)	
Accruals	(30,000)		(42,000)	
Working capital		16,000		81,000
Total Net assets		€244,000		€356,000
Financed by:				
Issued share capital		80,000		80,000
Profit and Loss balance		38,000		210,000
Long-term loan		126,000		66,000
		€244,000		€356,000

The stock at 1 January 1998 is €80,000.

Calculate each of the following ratios:

1. Working capital ratio

2. Liquidity ratio

3. Return on capital employed
4. Net profit %
5. Gross profit %
6. Stock turnover.

Comment on the significance of each of the ratios calculated.

EXERCISE 3

The following are the results of an electrical engineering business for y/e 31 December 1998 and 1999:

PROFIT AND LOSS ACCOUNT Y/E 31 DECEMBER

	1998	1999
	€	€
Sales	50,000	60,000
less Cost of sales	(34,000)	(42,000)
Gross profit	16,000	18,000
less Expenses	(14,300)	(17,700)
Net profit	€1,700	€300

BALANCE SHEET DETAILS FOR Y/E 31 DECEMBER

	1998	1999
	€	€
FIXED ASSETS	11,000	12,500
CURRENT ASSETS		
Stock	13,000	14,000
Debtors	15,000	16,000
Bank	500	500
CURRENT LIABILITIES		
Creditors	20,000	24,000

NOTE:

The stock at 1 January 1998 is €10,000.

Calculate the following ratios and comment on the position of the business for both years:

1. Working capital ratio
2. Liquidity ratio
3. Stock turnover
4. Gross profit %
5. Net profit %
6. Return on capital employed.

EXERCISE 4

The following information was extracted from two companies, both engaged in the same retail business of selling footwear:

	COMPANY A	COMPANY B
	€	€
Opening stock	6,000	10,500
Closing stock	6,400	9,000
Cost of sales	82,000	96,000
Sales	98,000	112,000
Expenses for year	5,000	6,700
Closing debtors	15,000	9,800

From the information given above, which of the companies do you consider to be in the better trading position? Use ratios to support your answer.

EXERCISE 5

The following information has been available from a trader for y/e 31 December 1999:

Working capital	€56,000
Current ratio	2 : 1
Liquidity ratio	1.7 : 1
Capital	€200,000
Debtors turnover	63 days
Gross profit %	40%
Net profit %	10%
Stock turnover	6 times
(based on closing stock)	
Fixed assets	€140,000

Current assets consist of stock, debtors and bank.

Current liabilities consist of creditors.

Prepare a Trading, Profit and Loss Account and Balance Sheet for y/e 31 December 1999 in as much detail as possible.

EXERCISE 6

The following are the results of two companies, A and B, for y/e 31 December 1999:

	COMPANY A	COMPANY B
	€	€
Sales	80,000	50,000
Cost of sales	36,000	14,000
Administration expenses	14,000	8,000
Selling expenses	2,000	1,500
Wages	4,000	3,500

Which of the above companies is the most profitable?

CHAPTER 9

Costing and Budgeting

Management accounting has been defined as the application of professional knowledge and skill to the preparation and presentation of accounting information in such a way as to assist management in the formulation of plans and policies. In other words, it is concerned with helping management to run a business effectively. While Financial accounting deals with the past, Management accounting is concerned with the present and future. The past is considered only insofar as it provides a guide as to what may happen in the future.

Cost accounting is concerned with the provision of information about costs and it is the essential foundation for the development of a Management accounting system.

Financial accounting is concerned with the historical recording of information, as we have already seen described in this book. It does not give management the detailed information necessary to enable it to control costs. Financial accounting produces a Profit and Loss Account without providing detailed information as to the composition of either revenue received or costs incurred. As a result, information provided by the Financial accounts is not sufficient for cost control and may be inappropriate for certain decision-making situations. This is where Management and Cost accounting are needed.

The following simplified account will give us some indication of the differences between Financial and Cost accounting systems:

TRADING, PROFIT AND LOSS ACCOUNT

	Debit €	Credit €
Sales		100,000
less Cost of sales:		
Materials used	50,000	
Production expenses	6,000	(56,000)
Gross profit		44,000
less Expenses:		
Wages	24,000	
Administration expenses	6,000	
Selling and distribution expenses	4,000	(34,000)
Net profit		€10,000

The above Financial account reveals to management that a Net profit of €10,000 has been made on sales of €100,000, which is 10% of sales. Where, however, the company is engaged in the production of more than one product, there is no indication of the costs associated with each product. Neither is there any indication of whether each product was profitable.

The cost accountant can provide more useful information to management as follows:

PRODUCT	A	B	C	D	TOTAL
	€	€	€	€	€
Sales	31,500	16,250	24,150	28,100	100,000
less Costs:					
Materials used	15,000	8,000	13,000	14,000	50,000
Production expenses	2,000	2,000	1,000	1,000	6,000
Wages	8,000	6,000	4,000	6,000	24,000
Administration expenses	1,400	1,600	1,500	1,500	6,000
Selling and distribution expenses	1,000	1,500	1,000	500	4,000
Total costs	27,400	19,100	20,500	23,000	90,000
Net profit	4,100	(2,850)	3,650	5,100	10,000

The management of the business can now see what the position is more clearly. It shows that Products A, C and D are profitable and that Product B has produced a loss.

With this information, management can make more efficient decisions. It may, for example,

- decide to stop producing Product B, or
- reduce the cost of Product B, or
- increase the unit selling price of Product B, or
- continue to produce and sell Product B as a 'loss leader'.

We can see from this example that Cost accounts can be more useful to management than Financial accounts in helping them make decisions. Cost accounts can provide the following:

- Disclosure of profitable and unprofitable lines of business.
- Control of waste by analysing the build-up of costs so that the causes for increases or decreases in profit/loss can be determined.
- Disclosure of the break-even point where the business makes neither profit or loss.
- Make or buy decisions: management can compare the cost of buying items with the cost of producing the same items themselves.
- Calculating selling prices. Where the market is extremely competitive, costing can ensure that orders are not lost through prices being too high. Costing will also ensure that prices are not being set unprofitably low.
- Future planning: cost information will assist management in deciding the best policy regarding the introduction of new machinery and equipment.
- Cost control: by comparing actual results against planned results, inefficiencies will be discovered and corrective action can be taken.

Elements of Cost

Costs can be divided into direct and indirect costs. **Direct costs** are those costs directly associated with producing a product that can be allocated to a particular cost unit, e.g. raw materials, direct labour. **Indirect costs** are those costs which cannot be easily allocated to a cost unit or product, e.g. indirect wages, administration expenses, selling expenses, etc.

Costs can also be classified into fixed and variable costs. **Fixed costs** are those costs that remain constant regardless of the number of units produced, for example, rates and insurance. **Variable costs** are those costs that change in direct proportion to the units produced, such as raw material costs and labour costs.

Marginal Costing

Marginal costing is a concept from economics. It is the amount by which, at any given volume of output, costs are changed if the volume is increased or decreased by one unit. Variable costs are included in the sales value and a contribution is calculated. In other words, the difference between the sales value of a product and its variable costs equals contribution. The fixed costs that are allocated to the product are deducted from the contribution to arrive at the Net profit of the product.

An example will help to emphasise this fact:

PRACTICE EXAMPLE 1

Roseberry Ltd makes a product with variable costs of €6 per unit and a selling price of €10 per unit. The production for the month of May was 10,000 units and fixed costs for the month were €22,500. Calculate the contribution and profit/loss on each of the following sales forecasts:

1.   5,000 units
2.   7,500 units
3.   10,000 units.

PRACTICE EXAMPLE 1 SOLUTION

1. 5,000 units sold:

Sales (at €10)	€50,000
less Variable costs (at €6)	(€30,000)
= Contribution	€20,000
less Fixed costs (remain constant)	(€22,500)
Net loss	(€2,500)

2. 7,500 units sold:

Sales (at €10)	€75,000
less Variable costs (at €6)	(€45,000)
= Contribution	€30,000
less Fixed costs (remain constant)	(€22,500)
Net profit	€7,500

3. 10,000 units sold:

Sales (at €10)	€100,000
less Variable costs (at €6)	(€60,000)
= Contribution	€40,000
less Fixed costs (remain constant)	(€22,500)
Net profit	€17,500

From the above example, we see that if only 5,000 units are sold the company will make a loss of €2,500. However, if 7,500 units are sold the company will make a profit of €7,500. Regardless of how many units are sold, the contribution per unit remains constant at €4. The contribution per unit is calculated by establishing the sales price per unit (€10) and subtracting the variable costs per unit (€6). The expected profit from the sales of 8,000 units would be:

Total contribution 8,000 units at €4 = €32,000
less Fixed costs (€22,500)
Net profit €9,500

From the above we can now state:

- If total contribution exceeds fixed costs, then a profit is made.
- If total contribution is less than fixed costs, there will be a loss.
- If total contribution exactly equals fixed costs, no profit or loss arises - break-even point is reached.

Let us review some terms and equations that are in common use in this area:

1. Total costs = Fixed costs + Variable costs
2. Contribution = Sales — Variable costs

   In other words, it is the amount left to contribute towards the fixed costs which still have to be met.
3. Profit = Contribution — Fixed costs
4. Contribution per unit = Sales per unit — Variable costs per unit
5. Break-even point = the level at which no profit is made nor loss suffered. It is the point at which fixed costs equal contribution.

The break-even point in units = $\dfrac{\text{Fixed costs}}{\text{Contribution per unit}}$

Returning to the example of Roseberry Ltd, how many units should the company sell in order to break-even?

$$\text{Break-even point} = \frac{\text{Fixed costs}}{\text{Contribution per unit}}$$

$$= \frac{€22,500}{€4}$$

= 5,625 units

If the company sells 5,625 units in the month, it will break-even, i.e. have no profit or loss. We can check our answer as follows:

5,625 units sold:
Sales (at €10) €56,250
less Variable costs (at €6) (€33,750)
= Contribution 22,500
less Fixed costs (remain constant) (€22,500)
Profit/loss nil

It follows from this that if the company sells more than 5,625 units in the month, it will be generating profit. If it sells less than 5,625 units, it will make a loss. This is useful information for management and it can be helpful in the following areas:

- Profit planning - for example, in measuring the contribution required of products.
- Product pricing - for example, fixing the selling price of a product.
- Make or buy decisions - whether to make products internally or whether to buy from outside suppliers.
- In determining the economic feasibility of major projects, such as the purchase of new machinery to produce a new product.

The Cost and Management accountant is concerned not only with recording costs, but also with the provision of information which will helpful when making decisions for the future. Management wants to know more than simply what profit is likely to be if the proposed production and sales levels are achieved. Management needs to know the point at which neither profit nor loss occurs the break-even point. It will also like to know the amount by which actual sales can fall below anticipated sales without a loss being incurred.

Where a company wishes to achieve a certain profit during a period, a formula may be applied to achieve this. Sales must cover all costs and leave the required profit.

Sales = Variable costs + Fixed costs + required Profit

Subtracting variable costs from both sides, we get:

Sales — Variable costs = Fixed costs + required Profit

Let us take another example to illustrate this point:

PRACTICE EXAMPLE 2

A business makes and sells a single product with variable costs of €12 per unit. The selling price is €15 per unit. Fixed costs per annum are €34,000. The objective of the business is to make a profit of €8,000 per annum. What sales are required to achieve this profit?

PRACTICE EXAMPLE 2 SOLUTION

Sales — Variable costs = Fixed costs + required Profit
Contribution = Fixed costs + required Profit
€42,000 = €34,000 + €8,000

The company needs a contribution of €42,000 per annum in order to cover fixed costs of €34,000 and have a profit of €8,000.

The contribution per unit = €15 — €12

= €3

Required sales = $\dfrac{€42,000}{3}$

= 14,000 units

Required sales volume   = 14,000 units at €15

                                     = €210,000

The company needs to sell 14,000 units in order to achieve a profit of €8,000 p.a.

Let us check our answer:

Sales = 14,000 units at €15	€210,000
less Variable costs = 14,000 units at €12	(€168,000)
= Contribution	€42,000
less Fixed costs	(€34,000)
Profit	€8,000

PRACTICE EXAMPLE 3

A company which produces a range of products has cost data for each product for the first time. The manager was surprised to discover that one of the products was making a loss. From the information shown below, calculate how many additional units of the product need to be sold in order to break-even:

Sales (2,000 units at €110 each)			€220,000
Direct labour		€100,000	
Direct materials		€40,000	
Factory overheads	- variable	€10,000	
	- fixed	€20,000	(€170,000)
			€50,000
Selling expenses	- variable	€32,000	
	- fixed	€15,000	
Other fixed overheads		€10,000	(€57,000)
Net loss			(€7,000)

PRACTICE EXAMPLE 3 SOLUTION

To calculate the break-even point, we must first distinguish between fixed and variable costs. All of the variable costs must be subtracted from the sales figure to arrive at contribution:

Sales (2,000 units at €110 each)			€220,000
less Variable costs			
Direct labour		€100,000	
Direct materials		€40,000	
Factory overheads	- variable	€10,000	
Selling expenses	- variable	€32,000	(€182,000)
= Contribution			€38,000
less Fixed costs:			
Factory overheads	- fixed	€20,000	
Selling expenses	- fixed	€15,000	
Others		€10,000	(€45,000)
Loss			(€7,000)

To break-even, we need to cover fixed costs of €45,000.

Total contribution on 2,000 units $= €38,000$

Contribution per unit $= \dfrac{€38,000}{2,000} = €19$

Break-even point $= \dfrac{\text{Fixed costs}}{\text{Contribution per unit}}$

$$= \dfrac{€45,000}{€19}$$

$$= 2,369 \text{ units}$$

Additional units to be sold are 2,369 units less 2,000 units i.e. 369 units.

Budgeting

A **budget** is a financial and/or quantitative plan of operations for the forthcoming accounting period. The control of budgets is the responsibility of management. It continuously compares actual and budgeted results to ensure the objectives of the company are attained.

For a system of budgetary control, there must be:

- Business objectives
- Allocation of responsibility
- Budgets
- Comparison of actual with budgeted results
- Corrective action.

The objectives and policies of the business will be set out in the long-term plan of the business. The budget will take the earliest period in this plan and develop it in more detail, making any necessary adjustments. Care must be taken here that decisions are not taken in the short-term which, while increasing profits within the budget period, will hinder the long-term objectives of the company.

The most common period for a budgets is one year, but there is no reason why this period cannot be either longer or shorter, depending on the requirements of the business. One of the purposes of producing a budget is to set targets with which actual performance can be compared. It is then possible to compare actual and budgeted figures and identify reasons for variations. To facilitate comparison, it is important that budgets should be produced in the same form as will be used for the accounts.

To produce a budget, it is first of all necessary to forecast future events which will influence the plans of the company. Secondly, sales and production in terms of revenues and costs must be forecast. Then the costs incurred in carrying out the activities must be identified, and also the revenues which will arise, in order to prepare the budget for the coming period.

Where a business has been in existence for a long time, costs and revenues can be projected by analysing past costs and revenues. But, of course, any major changes in the methods of operation or in products would have to be taken into account here since such changes will be reflected in future costs and revenues.

Preparing a Budget

The Sales budget is usually the first budget to be prepared. Without knowing our anticipated sales level, we cannot ascertain stocking and production requirements. In drawing up a Sales budget, the Sales manager will produce answers to the following questions:

- What products are to be sold?
- What amounts are to be sold?
- What prices are to be charged?

To arrive at answers, she will take account of the opinions and forecasts of the staff, any market research information available, and information on past performance and trends for the future.

The next step is to prepare the Production budget based on the anticipated sales for the budget period and the stocking levels required. When the required level of production is arrived at, other budgets can be prepared. For instance, the Labour expenses budget can be prepared. This will determine the labour usage and rates of pay required to meet budgeted production levels. Then the Expenses budget can be prepared. This will anticipate all the expenses necessary to achieve the required level of sales and production.

The final budget to be prepared is the Master budget. This incorporates all the figures from the other budgets and will include a budgeted Profit and Loss Account and Balance Sheet. It is only when the individual budgets are consolidated into the Master budget that it can be seen whether or not they are viable.

During the budget period, reports of actual results compared with budgeted results will be produced. Where the actual results differ from the budget, management's attention must be drawn to the significant variances. The management must then either take action to prevent the same variance arising in future, or if this is not possible due to outside circumstances, revise the budget accordingly.

Benefits of Budgetary Control

Budgets ensure that management plans for the future with a clear allocation of responsibilities. Without plans, the business would lack direction. Managers may become immersed in day-to-day operational problems to the detriment of the future.

Budgets provide a framework within which actual performance can be measured.

The analysis of variances draws immediate attention to the weaknesses of the business which may otherwise be overlooked.

The discipline of having to plan for the future facilitates better co-ordination between the activities of various departments within a business.

Limitations of Budgets

Budgets are not a substitute for action. What is the use in analysing variances if managers fail to take action?

Budgets can become so inflexible that they restrict initiative.

Cash Budgets

A Cash budget is concerned with liquidity, rather than profitability. A business needs not only to earn profits, but also to be able to pay debts as they fall due. A budget or forecast of cash requirements is therefore <u>advisable</u> in the ordinary course of trading and is <u>essential</u> where the company wants to make a decision regarding the expansion of capital expenditure.

A Cash budget is concerned with cash inflows and outflows. No account is taken of sales until the debtor pays, nor of purchases or other expenditure until the business pays the creditor. As the budget deals with future events, an estimate has to be made as to the average period of credit given to debtors and taken from creditors. A decision also has to be made as to the time span of the budget. Some companies may want a weekly cash budget but for others, a monthly budget would be adequate.

Cash inflows and outflows are netted off against each other to show the net cash inflow or outflow at a given point in time. This is especially useful for indicating the maximum bank overdraft a business will require during a period of expansion, pinpointing when this will occur. Similarly, it is advantageous to know whether the business will have cash surplus to its requirements. Surplus cash can then be invested profitably in short-term or long-term projects.

The method used in preparing a cash budget is to take the information available and convert it into a cash basis. These cash transactions are then listed for the shortest time basis being used. The totals are then summarised in the following format:

- Columns for months
- Rows for cash receipts and payments.

PRACTICE EXAMPLE 4

Alan Ltd commences business on 1 January with a cash balance of €2,000. From the following forecast information, prepare a monthly cash budget from January to June. Indicate the maximum overdraft required and when it will occur.

Purchases: €4,000 in January, €2,000 per month thereafter.

                  One month credit is taken from suppliers.

Sales: €3,000 per month.

                  Two months credit is given to customers.

Expenses: €200 per month, payable in the month incurred.

PRACTICE EXAMPLE 4 SOLUTION

CASH BUDGET FOR 6 MONTHS TO 30 JUNE

	Jan.	Feb.	Mar.	Apr	May	June
CASH INFLOW	€	€	€	€	€	€
Receipts from sales	-	-	3,000	3,000	3,000	3,000
Total Cash inflow	-	-	3,000	3,000	3,000	3,000
CASH OUTFLOW						
Payment for purchases	-	4,000	2,000	2,000	2,000	2,000
Expenses	200	200	200	200	200	200
Total Cash outflow	(200)	(4,200)	(2,200)	(2,200)	(2,200)	(2,200)
Net inflow/(outflow)	(200)	(4,200)	800	800	800	800
Opening balance	2,000	1,800	(2,400)	(1,600)	(800)	-
Closing balance	1,800	(2,400)	(1,600)	(800)	-	800

The maximum overdraft required will be in the region of €2,400 and will occur in February. Note carefully that neither sales nor purchases appear in the budget until cash changes hands at the end of the credit period e.g. sales made in January will not produce cash until March. Note also that the closing balance of cash for one month is the opening balance of cash for the next month.

Projected Trading, Profit and Loss Account

Profit may be defined as the difference between revenue and costs. A profit forecast is still the difference between revenue and costs, but forecast or estimated revenues and costs are used instead of actual amounts. The responsibility for making the forecast belongs to management but they may require the assistance of accountants. A profit forecast is incorporated into a budgeted or projected Trading, Profit and Loss Account.

From the Cash budget of Alan Ltd we looked at before, it is possible to construct a projected Trading, Profit and Loss Account and Balance Sheet from the information given, provided the figure for closing stock or the Mark up or Gross profit percentage is known. Mark up expresses the profit as a percentage of cost or purchase price. Gross profit percentage expresses the profit as a percentage of sales.

Assume in this case that the Gross profit % is 33.33%.

PROJECTED TRADING, PROFIT AND LOSS ACCOUNT OF ALAN LTD TO 30 JUNE

	Debit €	Credit €
Sales (€3,000 x 6 months)		18,000
less Cost of sales:		
Opening stock	-	
Purchases (€4,000 + €2,000 x 5 months)	14,000	
less Closing stock	(2,000)	
Cost of sales		(12,000)
Gross profit		6,000
less Expenses (€200 x 6 months)		(1,200)
Net profit		€4,800

NOTE: The Gross profit % is 33.33%. This means that the Gross profit is 33.33% of sales.

Sales	= €18,000
Gross profit 33.33%	= €6,000
Cost of sales	= €12,000

Therefore the closing stock must be €2,000. There is no opening stock as the business commenced trade on 1 January.

We can also draw up a projected Balance Sheet for the 6 months to 30 June:

PROJECTED BALANCE SHEET OF ALAN LTD TO 30 JUNE

	€	€
FIXED ASSETS		-
CURRENT ASSETS		
Closing stock	2,000	
Debtors	6,000	
Cash	800	
	8,800	
less CURRENT LIABILITIES		
Creditors	(2,000)	
Working capital		6,800
Total Net assets		€6,800
Financed by:		
Capital 1 Jan.	2,000	
add Net profit	4,800	
		€6,800

NOTE: Two months sales are outstanding which equals €3,000 x 2 months = €6,000.
One month purchases are outstanding which equals €2,000.

PRACTICE EXAMPLE 5

Doyle PLC was recently formed and intends commencing business on 1 July 2000. During the month of June 2000, the company will issue 600,000 ordinary shares at €1 each and the cash will be subscribed immediately and in full. Also during June, €390,000 will be spent on the purchase of plant and machinery and there will be an outlay of €150,000 on stock. This will leave a cash balance of €60,000 on 1 July 2000. Forecasts for the year beginning 1 July 2000 are as follows:

1. Stocks costing €120,000 will be sold each month at a mark up of 25%.
2. Debtors will be allowed 2 months credit.
3. Bad debts are estimated to be 2% of sales.
4. Month end stock levels will be maintained at €150,000 and creditors will allow 1 month credit.
5. Wages and other expenses will amount to €18,000 per month payable in the month incurred.
6. Plant and machinery will last for 5 years with no scrap value and depreciation will be on a straight-line basis.

Prepare a Cash budget for the company for July, August and September 2000 and show the maximum overdraft needed. Also prepare a projected Trading, Profit and Loss Account and Balance Sheet for y/e 30 June 2001.

PRACTICE EXAMPLE 5 SOLUTION

CASH BUDGET OF DOYLE PLC

	July €	August €	September €
CASH INFLOW			
Receipts from sales	-	-	147,000
Total Cash inflow	-	-	147,000
CASH OUTFLOW			
Payment for purchases	-	120,000	120,000
Wages and other expenses	18,000	18,000	18,000
Total Cash outflow	(18,000)	(138,000)	(138,000)
Net inflow/(outflow)	(18,000)	(138,000)	9,000
Opening balance	60,000	42,000	(96,000)
Closing balance	42,000	(96,000)	(87,000)

NOTES:

1.

Cost price of goods	€120,000
Mark up 25%	€30,000
= Sales	€150,000
less Bad debts 2%	(€3,000)
Cash received from sales	€147,000

2. The maximum overdraft needed is €96,000 in August 2000. In September 2000, this will be reduced by €9,000 to give an overdraft of €87,000. From September 2000 to the end of the accounting year, the overdraft will be reduced by €9,000 a month, leaving a bank overdraft of €6,000 at 30 June 2001.

PROJECTED TRADING, PROFIT AND LOSS ACCOUNT OF DOYLE PLC Y/E 30 JUNE 2001

	Debit €	Credit €
Sales (€150,000 x 12 months)		1,800,000
less Cost of sales:		
Opening stock	150,000	
Purchases (€120,000 x 12 months)	1,440,000	
	1,590,000	
less Closing stock	(150,000)	
Cost of sales		(1,440,000)
Gross profit		360,000
less expenses:		
Wages and other expenses (€18,000 x 12 months)	216,000	
Bad debts (€3,000 x 10 months)	30,000	
Provision for bad debts (€3,000 x 2 months)	6,000	
Depreciation plant and machinery (€390,000 at 20%)	78,000	(330,000)
Net profit		€30,000

PROJECTED BALANCE SHEET OF DOYLE PLC Y/E 30 JUNE 2001

	COST €	ACC. DEP. €	NBV €
FIXED ASSETS			
Plant and machinery	390,000	78,000	312,000
CURRENT ASSETS			
Stock		150,000	
Debtors (2 months sales)	300,000		
less Bad debts provision	(6,000)	294,000	
		444,000	
less CURRENT LIABILITIES			
Creditors (1 month purchases)	120,000		
Bank overdraft	6,000	(126,000)	
Working capital			318,000
Total Net assets			€630,000
Financed by:			
Issued share capital:			
600,000 ord. shares at €1 each			600,000
Reserves:			
Profit and Loss balance			30,000
			€630,000

Gross Profit Percentage and Mark Up

You must be clear about the difference between Gross profit percentage and Mark up.

Gross profit percentage or **Gross margin** expresses the Gross profit as a percentage of Sales. **Mark up** expresses the Gross profit as a percentage of the Cost of sales.

EXAMPLE 1

Sales for the period were €130,000. Gross profit % is 25%. Calculate the Gross profit figure and the Cost of sales figure.

Sales	= 100%	= €130,000
Gross profit	= 25%	= €32,500
Therefore Cost of sales		= €97,500

EXAMPLE 2

Sales for the period were €245,000. Mark up is 10%. Calculate the Gross profit and the Cost of sales.

Profit is 10% of the Cost of sales.

Cost of sales	=	100%
Profit	=	10%
Sales	=	110%
Sales	=	€245,000
Profit	=	$\dfrac{€245,000 \times 10}{110}$
	=	€22,273
Profit	=	€22,273
Cost of sales	=	€222,727

EXAMPLE 3

The Gross profit for the period is €20,000. Mark up is 20%. What are the Sales and Cost of sales figures?

Profit is 20% of the Cost of sales.

Cost of sales	=	100%
Profit	=	20%
Sales	=	120%
Cost of sales	=	$\dfrac{€20,000 \times 100}{20}$
	=	€100,000
Cost of sales	=	€100,000
Profit	=	€20,000
Sales	=	€120,000

EXAMPLE 4

The profit for the period is €35,000. The Gross profit % is 35%. What are the Sales and Cost of sales figures?

Profit is 35% of Sales.

Sales	=	100%
Profit	=	35%
Cost of sales	=	65%
Sales	=	$\dfrac{€35,000 \times 100}{35}$
	=	€100,000
Sales	=	€100,000
Profit	=	€35,000
Cost of Sales	=	€65,000

EXAMPLE 5

The Cost of sales for the period was €170,000. Gross profit % is 20%. What are the Sales and Gross profit figures?

Profit is 20% of sales.

Sales	=	100%
Profit	=	20%
Cost of sales	=	80%
Sales	=	$\dfrac{€170,000 \times 100}{80}$
	=	€212,500
Sales	=	€212,500
Cost of Sales	=	€170,000
Gross profit	=	€42,500

EXERCISE 1

Homelink Ltd has the capacity to produce 150,000 units per annum but last year's results were disappointing, as shown by the Trading, Profit and Loss Account below. They have asked for your help in determining how many units need to be sold in order to break-even.

TRADING, PROFIT AND LOSS ACCOUNT OF HOMELINK FOR Y/E 31 DEC 1999

		Debit	Credit
		€	€
Sales (90,000 units at €2)			180,000
less Cost of sales:			
Direct materials		45,000	
Direct labour		45,000	
Factory overheads	- variable	9,000	
	- fixed	40,000	(139,000)
Gross profit			41,000
Other expenses	- variable	13,500	
	- fixed	31,200	(43,700)
Net loss			(€2,700)

EXERCISE 2

Boyle Ltd manufactures Product X. A costing system is in operation and the forecast information is as follows:

Forecast labour rate €2 per hour

Forecast labour time 2 hours per unit.

During a period, the production figures revealed that 400 units of Product X were produced in 920 hours. The wage rate paid was €2.30 per hour.

You are required to compare the actual and budget figures for the labour rate and labour time and establish the variances, if any.

EXERCISE 3

You are managing a small printing company and you have been asked to quote for supplying 20,000 pamphlets. You budget for a Profit of 10% of sales. Costs are estimated to be:

Paper per 1,000 copies	€12
Wages per 1,000 copies	€8
Layout cost	€200 (for 20,000 copies)
Variable overheads	120% of wages
Fixed overheads	€80 (for 20,000 copies)

Prepare a cost computation showing the selling price to the nearest € that you would quote for 20,000 copies.

EXERCISE 4

Derel Ltd manufactures three products - A, B, and C. Sales revenue and costs have been budgeted as follows

	A €	B €	C €	TOTAL €
Sales revenue	60,000	80,000	40,000	180,000
Variable costs:	(40,000)	(60,000)	(34,000)	(134,000)
Fixed costs	(6,000)	(10,000)	(8,000)	(24,000)
Profit/(loss)	14,000	10,000	(2,000)	22,000

At present there is no possibility of increasing sales of any of the three products, nor of introducing any new product. The management are considering discontinuing Product C.

Should management discontinue Product C? Give reasons for your answer.

EXERCISE 5

The following is the Trading, Profit and Loss Account of York Ltd for y/e 31 December 1997.

	Debit €	Credit €
Sales (40,000 units at €2 each)		80,000
less Cost of sales:		
Direct materials	20,000	
Direct labour	10,000	
Factory overheads - variable	8,000	
- fixed	15,000	(53,000)
Gross profit		27,000
less other Expenses:		
Administration overheads - variable	4,000	
- fixed	2,500	
Selling expenses - variable	5,000	(11,500)
Net profit		€15,500

The company is contemplating increasing sales to 60,000 units, but to achieve this the selling price must be reduced by 10%. Because of the increased production, factory overhead fixed costs would increase by €5,000 and administration overhead fixed costs would increase by 20% due to the extra space needed.

Prepare a cost structure to determine whether the company should go ahead with the increased selling capacity.

EXERCISE 6

Mr Lyons has decided to commence business on 1 January 2000, with €30,000 cash introduced as Capital. Prior to visiting his bankers to secure more Capital, he requires you to produce a Cash budget, a projected Trading, Profit and Loss Account and a Balance Sheet for the first three months of operation. You ascertain the following information from him:

1. Projected sales income is as follows:

   January   €13,000
   February   €14,500
   March   €25,000

   All sales are for cash.

2. Purchases are as follows:

   January   €19,000
   February   €15,000
   March   €30,000

All purchases are on credit with one month credit taken from suppliers.

3. Drawings are to be €750 per month.

4. Rent amounts to €20,000 per annum, payable quarterly in advance.

5. Furniture and equipment costing €26,000 will be purchased in January.

6. Net wages amount to €2,000 per month after tax and PRSI and are payable in the month incurred. Tax and PRSI amount to 30% of gross wages, payable to the Revenue Commissioners in the month following the payment of wages.

7. Depreciation of furniture and equipment is calculated as 20% p.a. of cost.

8. The advertising budget is €3,600 spread equally over the year and payable monthly, one month in arrears.

9. Mr Lyons anticipates a Gross profit margin of 30%.

EXERCISE 7

Mr Carroll is contemplating going into business selling electrical goods. He has rented some small premises and he estimates that his costs will be as follows for the coming year:

Rent of premises   €10,000
Rates   €2,500
Telephone   €2,450
Light and heat   €2,300
Insurance   €800
Advertising   €450
Wages   €23,000
Sundries   €2,500

He wants to achieve a Gross profit % of 30%. What amount of sales would he need to generate in order to break-even?

What is the amount of sales he would need to generate in order to have a net profit of €15,000?

EXERCISE 8

Mr Smith has an order from a customer for 100,000 units of Product X. He is unsure of the selling price to charge. The cost structure is as follows:

Materials	€1.20 per unit
Other variable costs	50p per unit

Fixed costs allocated to 100,000 units are:

Rent and rates	€2,000
Administration expenses	€4,000
Other fixed overheads	€5,000

What is the selling price per unit Mr Smith must charge in order to break-even?

What selling price per unit must he charge in order to earn a profit of €20,000?

CHAPTER 10

SECTION C

Short Theory Questions

The following is a list of short theory questions that may arise in Section C of the NCVA Accounting/Accounts examination. Students should study these carefully and refer to the previous chapters in this book for guidance to the answers.

Question 1

What is meant by the double-entry principle of Bookkeeping? Give two examples of items that are recorded on the debit side of the ledger and two examples of items recorded on the credit side of the ledger.

Question 2

What is meant by the term Capital? How is it treated in the accounts? What are the transactions that increase and reduce the capital figure?

Question 3

What is a Trial Balance and what does it test?

Question 4

What does the Balance Sheet of a business record? What is the difference between a Trial Balance and a Balance Sheet?

Question 5

·What is the difference between Capital and Revenue expenditure? Give an example of each.

Question 6

Explain the following:

1. Fixed assets
2. Current assets
3. Current liabilities
4. Working capital.

Question 7

Define the term Depreciation. Explain the two most common methods of depreciation and give an example of each.

Question 8

What is meant by the 'accruals concept' of Accounting? Give an example of the application of the accruals concept.

Question 9
What is meant by the term 'provision for bad debts'? What is the double-entry to record the provision for bad debts?

Question 10
What is meant by a bad debt recovered? What is the double-entry to record a bad debt recovered?

Question 11
What is meant by the 'prudence concept'? Give an example in Accounting where the prudence concept applies.

Question 12
One of the characteristics of a company is that of a separate legal entity. What is meant by this statement?

Question 13
What are the main distinctions between a private and a public company?

Question 14
Most companies retain some of their profits. Why do they do this and what are retained profits used for?

Question 15
What is meant by the term 'appropriation of profit'?

Question 16
Explain the difference between the authorised and issued share capital of a company.

Question 17
What is meant by a Share premium?

Question 18
One of the main methods of borrowing by a company is in the form of a debenture loan. Give the characteristics of a debenture loan and name two types.

Question 19
What are the main distinctions between ordinary and preference shares of a company?

Question 20
Explain what is meant by 'intangible assets'. Give two examples.

Question 21
Stock is normally valued at the lower of cost or net realisable value. Explain what is meant by cost and net realisable value.

Question 22
Explain the difference between Gross margin and Mark up. Illustrate the difference with an example.

Question 23
What is meant by the liquidity of a business? What factors affect liquidity?

Question 24
What is meant by Financial Accounting and Management Accounting? Which type of Accounting is more useful to managers to run the day-to-day business of a company?

Question 25
What are the advantages of preparing a Cash Budget for a business?

PRACTICE EXAMINATION PAPER NO. 1
Accounting/Accounts NCVA Level 2

In this practice examination paper there are three sections as follows:

Section A: This contains one compulsory question on Final Accounts.

Section B: This contains two questions on ratios and costing. You must answer one question.

Section C: This contains short theory questions. You must answer two questions.

SECTION A

The following is a Trial Balance taken from the books of Hayes PLC as at 31 December 1999. The authorised share capital of the company is 400,000 ordinary shares at €1 each.

	Debit €	Credit €
Issued share capital: 280,000 ordinary shares at €1 each		280,000
Premises (cost €178,000)	150,000	
Machinery (cost €28,000)	20,000	
Motor vehicles (cost €25,000)	20,000	
Purchases and Sales	415,000	750,000
Returns	5,000	6,200
Profit and Loss balance 1/1/99		48,000
Debtors and Creditors	85,000	62,000
Stock 1/1/99	76,000	
Bank	190,000	
Cash on hand	1,400	
Salaries and wages	75,000	
Insurance	12,000	
Discounts	4,000	6,500
Rent and rates	4,500	
Provision for bad debts		4,000
Light and heat	5,000	
Bank charges	1,500	
Carriage in	700	
Customs duties	400	
Carriage out	1,950	
Bills receivable and bills payable	19,000	5,000
Administration expenses	14,550	
Legal fees	1,500	
Directors' fees	26,700	
Commissions	2,800	
Goodwill	60,000	
Share premium account		50,000
Debenture interest	4,000	
Investments (market value €80,000)	85,000	
Investment income		8,000
Bad debts	1,200	
Rent receivable		2,000
Preliminary expenses	1,500	
10% Debentures		62,000
	€1,283,700	€1,283,700

The following information is also available:

1. Stock at 31 December 1999 is valued at cost, €65,000. Its market value is €80,000.
2. Provide for directors' fees due of €1,300.
3. The bad debts provision is to be adjusted to 5% of debtors.
4. Provide for light and heat due of €800.
5. The figure for rent and rates is for the 15 month period to 31 March 2001.
6. Provide for debenture interest outstanding.
7. Depreciation is to be provided as follows:

   Premises - 2% p.a. on cost,
   Machinery - 10% p.a. on cost,
   Motor vehicles - 20% p.a. reducing balance.

8. An extension to the premises has been added during the year. The cost of labour, €8,000, is included in the figure for salaries and wages. The materials, costing €12,000, were taken from the firm's own stocks. No adjustment has been made in the accounts.
9. All expenses in the Profit and Loss Account should be classified under the headings of a) Administration and Establishment, b) Selling and Distribution, and c) Financial.

Prepare a Trading, Profit and Loss Account and Balance Sheet of Hayes PLC for y/e 31 December 1999.

SECTION B

Answer one of the following questions:

Question 1

The following figures were taken from the books of Pipe Ltd.

	y/e 31/12/98	y/e 31/12/99
	€	€
Current assets	65,000	85,000
Closing stock	15,000	12,000
Net profit	68,000	73,000
Gross profit	120,000	148,000
Purchases	86,000	108,000
Sales	200,000	280,000
Total capital employed	300,000	350,000
Current liabilities	28,000	24,000

The stock at 1 January 1998 is €10,000.

Calculate each of the following ratios and comment on the performance of Pipe Ltd in terms of liquidity and profitability.

a) Gross profit %
b) Net profit %
c) Return on capital employed
d) Stock turnover
e) Working capital ratio
f) Liquidity ratio.

Question 2

The following is the Trading, Profit and Loss Account of Mr Dooley for y/e 31 December 1999:

	Debit €	Credit €
Sales (400,000 units at €1 each)		400,000
less Cost of sales:		
Direct materials	200,000	
Direct labour	40,000	
Other variable overheads	10,000	(250,000)
Gross profit		150,000
less other Expenses:		
Administration overheads - variable	5,000	
- fixed	25,000	
Selling expenses - variable	10,000	
- fixed	20,000	(60,000)
Net profit		€90,000

For the year 2000, Mr Dooley is contemplating increasing sales to 800,000 units, but if this occurs, the selling price would have to be reduced by 10%. In order to meet the increased production, Mr Dooley would require an extra factory. This factory would cost €400,000 and would be depreciated by 5% p.a. straight-line. Administration overhead fixed costs would increase by 20% and fixed selling costs would increase by 25%.

Prepare a cost computation to determine whether Mr Dooley should go ahead with the increased selling capacity.

SECTION C

Answer two of the following questions:

Question 1

What is meant by depreciation of fixed assets? Give an example illustrating the two main methods of depreciation.

Question 2

What is the difference between ordinary and preference shares?

Question 3

Necessary adjustments have to be made in Final Accounts to allow for accruals and prepayments. What is meant by an accrual and a prepayment and state how they are treated in the Final Accounts of a business.

PRACTICE EXAMINATION PAPER NO. 2
Accounting/Accounts NCVA Level 2

Section A: This contains one question on Final Accounts, which is compulsory.

Section B: This contains two questions. You must answer one question.

Section C: Short theory questions. You must answer two questions.

SECTION A

The following is the Trial Balance of Brown PLC as at 31 December 1999. The authorised share capital of the company is 380,000 ordinary shares at €1 each.

	Debit €	Credit €
Issued share capital: 350,000 ordinary shares at €1 each		350,000
Profit and Loss balance, 1/1/99	50,000	
Purchases	327,000	
Sales		790,000
Returns	4,000	2,000
Land	200,000	
Premises (cost €225,000)	200,000	
Motor vehicles (cost €80,000)	60,000	
Goodwill	25,000	
10% Investments (market value €80,000)	90,000	
Investment income		7,000
Bank		28,500
Salaries and wages	63,000	
Advertising	20,000	
Discounts	3,500	6,250
Debtors	78,000	
Creditors		45,000
Stock 1/1/99	82,000	
Provision for bad debts		2,250
Rent	18,500	
Bills receivable and bills payable	4,000	7,750
General expenses	22,000	
Bank term loan		36,000
Bank charges	800	
Light and heat	23,000	
Carriage in	4,450	
Carriage out	3,000	
Import duties	900	
Debenture interest	6,000	
10% Debentures		80,000
Bad debts written off	2,250	
Administration expenses	28,000	
Directors' fees	72,000	
Share premium account		32,650
	€1,387,400	€1,387,400

The following information is also available:

1. Stock at 31 December 1999 is valued at €94,000 cost. The market value of this stock is €108,000.
2. The provision for bad debts is to be adjusted to 5% of debtors.
3. Provide for debenture interest and investment income outstanding.
4. The rent figure includes a payment of €3,700 for the period 1 January to 31 March 2000.
5. General expenses includes an amount of €4,000 for the period to 31 March, 2000.
6. Advertising prepaid is €2,500.
7. Depreciation is to be provided as follows:

    Premises - 2% p.a. on cost.
    Motor vehicles - 10% p.a. on net book value.

Prepare a Trading, Profit and Loss Account and Balance Sheet of Brown PLC for y/e 31 December 1999.

SECTION B

Answer one of the following questions:

Question 1

The following figures were taken from the books of Bland Ltd for the years 1998 and 1999:

	y/e 31/12/98	y/e 31/12/99
	€	€
Current liabilities	26,000	24,000
Current assets	84,000	82,000
Closing stock	24,000	21,000
Net profit	60,000	80,000
Cost of sales	186,000	240,000
Gross profit	50,000	72,000
Capital employed	185,000	200,000

Calculate the following for y/e 31 December 1999:

a) Purchases
b) Return on capital employed
c) Net profit %
d) Stock turnover
e) Liquidity ratio.

Comment on the performance of Bland Ltd in terms of liquidity and profitability.

Question 2

The following is the Trading, Profit and Loss Account of Macro Ltd for y/e 31 December 1999:

	Debit	Credit
	€	€
Sales (350,000 units at €1 each)		350,000
less:		
Raw materials used	80,000	
Factory overheads	44,000	
Wages	41,000	
Selling expenses	18,000	
Depreciation	8,000	
		(191,000)
Net profit		€159,000

For the year 2000, the company is contemplating increasing sales to 700,000 units, but the selling price would have to be reduced by 10%. In order to achieve the increased turnover, management has the following alternatives:

(a) Rent an extra factory to accommodate the increased production levels. This would add an extra €40,000 onto the factory overhead expenses and it would double the depreciation charge. There would be extra administration expenses of €8,000. Wages would increase by 60%.

(b) Accommodate the increased production levels in the existing factory by introducing a second shift. Wages for the second shift would be 30% higher than the first shift. Extra administration expenses would be €6,000. Depreciation and factory overheads would remain as for 1999.

For both alternatives, the selling expenses will increase by 20% in 2000 and the price of raw materials will increase by 10%.

Prepare a cost computation to determine which is the best alternative for Macro Ltd. Briefly comment on the results disclosed.

SECTION C

Answer two of the following questions:

Question 1

What is meant by a bad debts provision? Show how an increase in a bad debts provision is treated in Accounting.

Question 2

What is the difference between capital and revenue expenditure? Give an example of each.

Question 3

What is the difference between the authorised and issued share capital of a company?

PRACTICE EXAMINATION PAPER NO. 3
Accounting/Accounts NCVA Level 2

In this practice examination paper, there are three sections as follows;

Section A: This contains one compulsory question on Final Accounts.

Section B: This contains two questions. You must answer one question.

Section C: This contains short theory questions. You must answer two questions.

SECTION A

The following is a Trial Balance of Harty PLC for y/e 31 December 1999. The authorised share capital of the company is 270,000 ordinary shares at €1 each.

	Debit €	Credit €
Ordinary share capital (€1 shares)		250,000
Premises (cost €200,000)	180,000	
Equipment (cost €50,000)	40,000	
Motor vehicles (cost €158,000)	120,000	
Profit and Loss balance 1/1/99		68,000
Purchases and Sales	317,000	680,000
Returns	4,400	3,000
Goodwill	20,000	
Patents and trade marks	8,000	
Carriage in	12,000	
Debtors and Creditors	86,000	24,000
Stock 1/1/99	42,000	
Cash on hand	3,300	
Bank	44,000	
Insurance	12,500	
Discounts	4,800	1,400
Provision for bad debts		2,250
Rent and rates	15,000	
Advertising	1,500	
Carriage out	1,800	
10% Investments (market value €80,000)	50,000	
Bad debts	2,850	
Directors' fees	48,000	
Administration expenses	26,500	
Commissions	22,000	
Rent receivable		14,000
Bills receivable and bills payable	19,000	14,000
Legal fees	4,000	
Bank charges	800	
Light and heat	2,300	
Bank term loan		45,000
Share premium account		50,000
Debenture interest	2,900	
8% Debentures		60,000
Salaries and wages	126,000	
Investment income		5,000
	€1,216,650	€1,216,650

The following information is also available:

1. Stock at 31 December 1999 is valued at €34,000.

2. The debtors figure includes an amount of €950 which is to be written off as a bad debt. The provision for bad debts is to be adjusted to 4% of debtors.

3. Outstanding debenture interest is to be provided for.

4. The rent and rates figure in the Trial Balance is for the 15 month period to 31 March 2000.

5. Provide for insurance prepaid of €2,500.

6. Provide for rent receivable due of €1,200.

7. Depreciation is to be provided as follows:

    Premises - 2% p.a. on cost.
    Equipment - 10% p.a. on cost.
    Motor vehicles - 20% p.a. reducing balance method.

Prepare a Trading, Profit and Loss Account and Balance Sheet of Harty PLC for y/e 31 December 1999.

SECTION B

Answer one of the following questions:

Question 1

The following information is supplied by James Murphy for the y/e 31 December 1999:.

Opening Capital	€500,000
Stock turnover (based on closing stock)	6 times
Net profit	€40,000
Mark up	33.3%
Current assets	€130,000
Working capital ratio	2:1
Period of credit given to debtors	1 month
Drawings	€60,000
Total expenses	€20,000

Current assets consist of stock, debtors and bank.

Creditors is the only current liability.

Prepare a Trading, Profit and Loss Account and Balance Sheet of James Murphy for y/e 31 December 1999 in as much detail as possible.

Question 2

A business wishes to supply 50,000 units of Product X to a customer. The owner is unsure of the selling price to charge. The costs associated with Product X are as follows:

Materials	€1 per unit
Other variable costs	30c per unit

Fixed costs allocated to 50,000 units are:

Rent and rates	€4,000
Insurance and depreciation	€1,000
Other fixed costs	€3,000

What selling price must the business charge in order to break-even on the sale of 50,000 units of Product X?

What selling price must it charge in order to make a profit of €7,500?

SECTION C

Answer any two of the following questions:

Question 1

What is a debenture loan? Describe its characteristics and list two types.

Question 2

What is meant by the 'prudence concept'? Give an example in Accounting where the prudence concept applies.

Question 3

What is meant by intangible assets? Give two examples.